What People Are Saying About *Insatiable*

"This book was very enjoyable to read because it showed me how my peers suffer. While reading this, I felt I was learning what problems and consequences I'm going to experience. It gave me a very vivid image of the disadvantages of eating disorders. It is an unpredictable story that created many feelings about the ongoing problem."

—Cat Bosmeny
age 12

"A poignant, true and telling account, written beautifully, empathically and memorably. This is a superb book that tells the truth but also offers hope."

—Edward M. Hallowell, M.D.
director of The Hallowell Center for Cognitive and Emotional Health
bestselling author of *Connect* and *Worry*

"An exquisitely crafted tale of four girls, their friends, their parents, their boyfriends and their relationships with food. A must-read for anyone interested in what it is like when food becomes your best friend or your worst enemy. Fantastically inspiring, a real page-turner. So fresh. I have never read anything at all like it."

—Mary Bertsch, C.A.S.A.C.

"Eve Eliot has written a 'classic' book that is compelling and significant in revealing the downward spiral to which eating disorders and self-mutilation lead. Encompassing the issues of self-worth, self-hate, family dynamics, and psychosocial and spiritual foundations, this book illustrates their interrelationships in an enlightening way.

"Written in a descriptive and conversational style, and told through the eyes, hearts, souls and guts of those with eating disorders, *Insatiable* is a gripping novel. It is also an outstanding resource that should be a part of public, high-school, college and medical-school libraries, and an integral part of the counselor-education course curriculum.

"This book speaks volumes in its mission for healing eating and self-mutilation disorders. A literary masterpiece!"

—Myrna M. Taylor, R.N., B.S., M.A.
Tucson, AZ

"As a parent, I appreciated finding a book for teenagers that demystifies the world of eating disorders. In a very comfortable and nonthreatening style, this book helps teens discover that they are not alone in their struggle, and that with treatment and support, recovery and self-happiness are possible. Hats off to Ms. Eliot for tackling an important topic in a sensitive and creative way."

—Lauren Bosmeny
mother of four

"As a grandmother of eight, reading this book has made me aware that there is help for teenagers with eating disorders. Society has put such pressure on these kids that they need to know they're not alone."

—Joan Cirrito
Tucson, AZ

Insatiable

The Compelling Story of Four Teens, Food and Its Power

EVE ELIOT

HCI TEENS

Health Communications, Inc.
Deerfield Beach, Florida

www.hci-online.com

Library of Congress Cataloging-in-Publication Data

Eliot, Eve, date.
    Insatiable : the compelling story of four teens, food, and its power /
Eve Eliot.
        p.   cm.
    ISBN 1-55874-818-0 (trade paper)
    1. Eating disorders in adolescence. 2. Eating disorders—Patients.
3. Teenagers—Mental health. 4. Body image. I. Title

RJ506.E18 E44 2001
616.85'26'00835—dc21

00-049865

Publisher: Health Communications, Inc.
            3201 S.W. 15th Street
            Deerfield Beach, FL 33442-8190

Cover and inside book design by Lawna Patterson Oldfield
Front cover photo by John Foxx Photography ©2000
Author photo by James Del Grosso

Dedicated,

with love and thanks,

to all my clients, past and present.

You know who you are.

You could spend your whole life
being a bell, and never know it,
'til something strikes you
and you ring.

—Anonymous

INSATIABLE

Samantha's heart nearly stopped as she realized what Brian was actually telling her. Because there were other students all around them, milling past carrying books and backpacks, she forced herself to breathe evenly, to look normal, perfect as always. This was what was expected of her, the blondest cheerleader with the cutest boyfriend, the prettiest girl at Maple Ridge High.

Brian sat with one ankle resting on his knee, leaning forward to allow her to hear him, speaking in low tones so nobody else could. He had one hand on his knee, one on his ankle. Samantha focused on the pattern of prominent blue veins in his big square hands, on his long fingers, on the sole of his work boot, on the pebbles and twigs that had become embedded in the grooved sole, on anything but his words.

A midriff appeared directly in front of Samantha. The midriff was encased in a tight, white T-shirt. It belonged to Polly Milkins, the only girl in school whose beauty Samantha feared.

"Hi, Sam," said Polly. "Will I see you at cheerleading practice later?"

"Sure," replied Samantha, turning to look up and organizing her face into its most radiant smile.

"Hi, Brian," said Polly, giggling a little. This was the effect Brian had on girls everywhere, this excitement that usually made them giggle.

"Hi, Polly." Brian looked at Polly briefly, then cleared his throat and uncrossed his legs. A brief, awkward silence ensued.

"Well—okay. Later," Polly said finally.

At the same time that Polly turned to walk across the athletic field toward the gym, Brian leaned back, far away from Samantha. At that moment, it seemed as though Brian had pulled far, far away, beyond the distance spanned by the parking lot, beyond the new gym with its gleaming windows, beyond the end of the road to where the street disappeared into the entrance to the bird sanctuary, beyond her reach entirely. He looked down at his feet. He dug the toe of one work boot into the ground, smashing the grass into liquid, green sludge.

In the village of Leeswood, thirty-five miles to the west, Hannah Bonanti sat on her bed reading *Baking for Health* and listening to her favorite band, Dracula Jones.

> *A dead-end road off a one-way street,*
> *When I get back home I'll never leave.*

They were an upstate band who'd played at a club in New York City on a night when Hannah's friends, Tanya and Kaneesha, had taken her out for her sixteenth birthday. Their rhythmic guitars pounded as Hannah read corn muffin recipes. Baking was a tradition among the women in Hannah's family. Hannah's mother had died two years before. Whenever Hannah felt lonely, sad, or anxious, reading this book, which had been her mom's, helped connect her with her mother.

It was Friday and the spring term (finally) was coming to an end. She had spent the afternoon hanging out with Kaneesha and Tanya. They had talked about going to see the new Tom Cruise movie at the mall.

Hannah wore her favorite jeans and a tank top that matched her gray eyes. She had painted her nails bright, iridescent green. Toenails, also green, peeked out of the open toes of her new black wedgies. It was 7:35. Where were they? Now that Kaneesha had her regular license, she was going to pick up Hannah in her dad's new black Chrysler Sebring.

Tanya and Kaneesha lived alone with their dad, too. Hannah felt comforted that she wasn't the only girl she knew in that situation. Kaneesha's mother hadn't died, though; she had taken off with Kaneesha's uncle.

Kaneesha had made Hannah feel welcome from the first day they'd met in Spanish class. Kaneesha had remarked, *"Buenas dias, me gusta tu tatuaje,"* telling Hannah—completely in Spanish—that she liked her tattoo, and their friendship had grown from that point on. Hannah loved Kaneesha's sense of fun; her beautiful, chocolate skin; her long, graceful, muscular arms; and the curly lashes that framed her dark, upward-slanting eyes. Tanya was Kaneesha's older sister.

But where were they? It was 7:45 already, and the movie started at 8:10.

* * *

Sixty-six miles east of where Hannah waited for her friends, Jessica Blaine sat on a stool in her green kitchen, talking to Phoebe McIntyre on the phone. Though only sixteen, Jessica's voice had a gravelly quality usually associated with middle-aged women who have smoked two packs of cigarettes a day for twenty years. Though Jessica had smoked Marlboros since the age of twelve, even as a baby her voice had sounded harsh.

Earlier that day, two girls in Jessica's math class had come up to her and remarked, "Only you could wear red plaid leggings with a striped T-shirt. How do you get away with it? And how do you keep your stomach so flat? We think we hate you, Jess!"

Tall, pale and very thin, she sat with her long, brown hair piled on top of her head, her legs crossed, smoking, looking out the window at her six-year-old brother Matthew's swing set. She wore a watch with big, glow-in-the-dark yellow numerals and a red plastic strap. Matthew had given her the watch the previous Christmas. He sat at her feet, building a Lego hospital. Beside her, glass-fronted cabinets held her mother's angel collection, along with the useful equipment of the family's everyday life.

Jessica had lately begun to attract the attention of her teachers because of her increasingly emaciated appearance.

She was skipping English class because it was on the second floor, and she couldn't climb stairs anymore without feeling dizzy. She appreciated the fact that she lived in a ranch house.

Other girls at school envied her. So many of them came up to her in the hall and told her how great she looked, asking how she stayed so thin. Phoebe had just asked her this, in fact.

"Try cutting out the fat," Jessica answered. "You can still eat stuff, but cut the fat way down and you'll get thin, you'll see." She jumped off the stool and walked into the hall to admire herself in the mirror.

"Well, what about pizza?" asked Phoebe, in a pouting tone. "Can't I have that?"

"No," warned Jessica, looking at herself from the side. She smoothed her palm over her flat stomach, gazing with satisfaction at the sharp angle of her jawline and then at the narrowness of her thighs in their plaid leggings.

"My dad says I need therapy," said Phoebe. "He says I have hand-to-mouth disease."

"Whatever," said Jessica, turning to look at herself from the other side.

Her Limp Bizkit CD reversed itself. Her admiration for herself swelled. She could feel that familiar glow of self-satisfaction spreading from her heart in radiating arcs of warmth.

"You can't attract a boy like Daryl if you're going to eat pizza," said Jessica sternly.

"But I can't even imagine life without pizza," wailed Phoebe.

"It's a trade-off," said Jessica. One thing everyone knew about Jessica—besides how thin she was—she was blunt.

Phoebe sighed. "I can't stand the idea of not eating things I like." She felt hopeless, helpless and alone.

Phoebe looked despairingly at the posters of Audrey Hepburn, which covered the walls of her room. She felt there was nothing special about herself; Jessica, on the other hand, had everything. She was not only gorgeous and a cheerleader, she was skinny and an artist, too. Jessica's room was filled with fashion drawings she had done. The flowing lines and skillful, colored-pencil sketches of clothes showed talent. She had designed entire ensembles, including hair-styles and accessories—shoes, handbags and jewelry. Her style combined a feel for medieval fashion with "trekky," space-age accents, which Phoebe ached to be able to wear herself.

Now, Jessica wore a laced silver-lamé bustier she had made herself, paired with plaid leggings and chunky silver platforms.

"You have to try harder, Phoeb," insisted Jessica, as she walked down the hall to her bedroom. She hunched up her shoulder to press it against the white phone so that she could use both hands to take a stack of magazines off a high shelf.

"How do you not eat when you're so hungry you could kill?" asked Phoebe.

"I tell myself that hunger isn't as horrible as the fat is," answered Jessica. "I tell myself how happy I'll feel when I wake up tomorrow morning feeling clean and thin."

She sat down on her white bedspread appliquéd with little Harley-Davidsons, which she had made herself, turning the pages of magazines bearing photos of tall young women as thin as she. They were wearing impractical clothes in glamorous settings. One girl wore a long yellow chiffon skirt over a teal bikini. She stood, her tan glorious and golden, on a wide beach, beneath a palm tree whose leaves were ruffled by a Caribbean breeze. Long-legged, not much older than Jessica, the model looked like an exotic flower. Jessica felt she was exotic, also. She didn't have needs like other people. She could refuse food. She was proud of this. She could say no to tacos and chocolate and fried-chicken dinners.

"I tell myself how special I am," said Jessica. "I tell myself I'm different because I can be hungry and still not eat."

* * *

Hannah Bonanti dialed Kaneesha's number at 8:30, then again at 8:45. She sat locked in her peaches-and-cream–colored bedroom, surrounded by the remains of her most recent binge: Mars Bars wrappers; empty pint cartons of Edy's triple-chocolate ice cream; a few empty bags of Chips Ahoy cookies, only smudges of chocolate and a few crumbs left inside; two crumpled empty bags of baked Lay's potato chips; and a jar with Mr. Peanut on it that had contained cashew nuts.

She had eaten continuously—and quickly—for forty-five minutes, and only when her stomach was so bloated that it hurt was she compelled to stop. She felt so hungry, but no matter how many pieces of fried chicken or jars of peanut butter Hannah stuffed into herself, she did not feel satisfied or settled or safe. She only felt more disgusted. She felt like dying . . . or throwing up. Just as she was planning to do the latter, though, her father came home.

Tony Bonanti, who had a clothing-manufacturing company in New York City, worked long hours and often came home as late as 9:00.

As she heard her father's car pull up, Hannah hastily shoved the binge remains under her bed, making sure the bedspread concealed them, then unlocked her door.

"Weren't you going out with Kaneesha and Tanya tonight,

honey?" he asked, surprised to see her in her room as he walked past it. He was a silver-haired man, with a bouncy, athletic walk.

"I got stood up," sighed Hannah dejectedly.

"Kaneesha wouldn't do that," said her father, unknotting his tie with his left hand as he sat on her bed to put his arm around her shoulder.

"Well, she did," said Hannah.

Hannah leaned against her dad and smelled his familiar scent of Old Spice and cigars. It was this scent she remembered most vividly the day her mother had gotten the results of her breast biopsy. The three of them had been in the kitchen. When her mother had put down the phone, her stricken look had told them everything. Her father held her mother, and they'd stood in the kitchen, all three of them, swaying together as the tears and fears welled up and finally flowed.

Hannah pulled herself upright and felt for the four gold studs she wore in her left ear, reassuring herself that they were still there. *How could they do this to me?* thought Hannah angrily.

"What do you think happened?" asked her father, turning toward her.

Hannah could see the worry in his gray eyes. "They forgot me, I guess."

"They didn't forget you," he said. "They probably just misunderstood the time."

Hannah's jeans felt uncomfortably tight. She suddenly felt tears springing out of her eyes. They rolled down her cheeks, streaking her blush.

"Oh, Han," said her father as he held her.

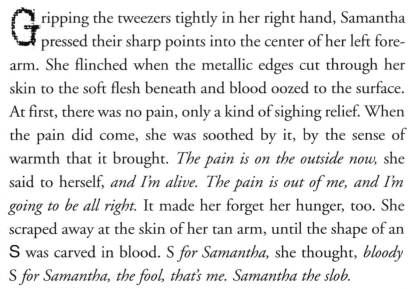

Gripping the tweezers tightly in her right hand, Samantha pressed their sharp points into the center of her left forearm. She flinched when the metallic edges cut through her skin to the soft flesh beneath and blood oozed to the surface. At first, there was no pain, only a kind of sighing relief. When the pain did come, she was soothed by it, by the sense of warmth that it brought. *The pain is on the outside now,* she said to herself, *and I'm alive. The pain is out of me, and I'm going to be all right.* It made her forget her hunger, too. She scraped away at the skin of her tan arm, until the shape of an **S** was carved in blood. S *for Samantha,* she thought, *bloody* S *for Samantha, the fool, that's me. Samantha the slob.*

A drop of blood fell from the tip of the tweezers onto her

zebra-patterned bedspread, its scarlet gleam looking startling against the starkness of the bedspread's black and white. She quickly wiped the blood away, though it left a tiny, brownish mark.

Samantha looked around her room, the sun illuminating the shelf of trophies she'd won for track. She loved running; it felt like flying. The shelf below the trophies held Samantha's zebra collection: soft stuffed zebras and shiny porcelain ones, zebras carved out of African wood, and framed crayon drawings of zebras she'd made as a little girl. One zebra, smallish relative to the grasses around it, looked straight out of the paper, scared by a thunderclap. Samantha looked at her new wound, then walked into the large red-and-white–tiled bathroom that adjoined her bedroom. She patted her injured arm with a gauze pad soaked in peroxide and placed a bandage over her handiwork. The blue plastic Band-Aid was printed with red stars, white moons and yellow planets. She slipped on a long-sleeved black T-shirt.

Samantha felt much better after she cut herself. At least she'd done something, and whatever was bad about her, whatever had made Brian leave, had been properly punished. Now maybe everything would be all right. Now maybe they could start over. It was spring, the season of new starts. Samantha's friend, Alexa, thought Brian did have a point; Samantha did eat very little. *But what does*

Alexa know? Samantha thought. Her friend Jenna thought maybe Brian just needed some time to cool down.

Samantha pushed her blond bangs out of her eyes. She scrutinized her complexion in the mirror below the harsh, unforgiving bathroom light, looking for the flaws that often afflicted sixteen-year-old complexions. Freckles sprinkled her forehead and nose in just exactly the right places. There were no imperfections, none at all. Her face was smooth and radiant, framed by shining, yellow-blond hair that fell straight to her shoulders. She sighed with relief. It always amazed her that none of the pain or tiredness she felt showed in her face, but there was something like sadness in her green eyes.

Her mother would want to know what had happened to Samantha's arm if she ever got a look at it. This was not the first time Samantha had cut herself, and she was good at inventing stories about these wounds. She would tell her mother that she'd been splattered with cooking oil at the pizza place where she worked on weekends. Her mother would also want to know if she'd eaten anything that day, and Samantha would lie about that, too. She'd tell her mother that she'd eaten breakfast at her friend's house, where she had spent the night. In fact, she hadn't eaten anything at all since two days earlier, when she'd been so hungry she surrendered to a fat-free bran muffin, eating it furtively, like a raccoon in the dark recesses of a hollowed-out tree. She wouldn't even think of eating pizza anymore; that was out of the question. She thought about her plump friend, Alexa, with fear and disgust: that double chin, those puffy cheeks, that soft, billowy body. She couldn't imagine letting herself get that fat—ever.

People were not the only things that could be fat. Rooms could be fat, too. Unmade beds and books not lined up in order of size could be fat, and the fatness could rub off on you.

"Sam," called her mother from the other side of the door to Samantha's room, "come spend some time with us. You use this house as if it's a hotel."

"I'll be right down," said Samantha dejectedly, sliding wearily off her bed.

She smoothed the surface of her zebra-patterned bedspread and surveyed the results. Orderliness was very important to her. When her room was vacuumed and the zebras were arranged all in a neat row, and when she hadn't eaten in a whole day, life was bearable and the world seemed like a safe and predictable place. But, every now and then, even with these small bits of magic in place, Samantha experienced the world as she knew it really was: a harsh, unpredictable place where terrible things could happen in the next moment, and no amount of vacuuming or starving could stave them off.

She took a last look at herself in her full-length mirror.

Her lovely heart-shaped face, with its pointy chin and full lips, did not reveal the loneliness, confusion and fear she felt. She frowned as she turned to look at herself from the side, placing her hand over her flat belly disapprovingly. Somehow, it was never flat enough, and she was never pretty enough or thin enough or smart enough. That was proven this morning, when Brian had told her he was tired of being with a girl who cared more about how she looked than about going to parties; a girl who was afraid of going to parties because there'd be food there that she might be tempted to eat. He didn't understand how hard it was to be her. No one did.

"Sam, I just feel so unhappy for you," Brian had said, looking at her with those incredible eyes, eyes that had once seemed so tender, but now were hard and indifferent to her. "But I just don't feel that we're, I don't know, normal together. You're always so worried about food and your weight and everything. It makes me feel bad about myself, not being able to help you." He seemed sad, but also relieved, Sam thought, as he turned and walked down the hall to his English class.

Samantha had known Brian since seventh grade. She had enjoyed being with him because he seemed to under-stand that she was different, more fragile than other girls in some way. If only she was thinner, she thought, Brian would come back. She would get thinner and thinner, and everyone at Maple Ridge High would notice, and then Brian would realize what a terrible mistake he had made, and he would come back.

She pulled on her zebra-striped leggings and gave her black T-shirt a final inspection to make sure it had no bits of lint clinging to it. Then she turned away from the mirror and, giving her bangs a final fluff, stepped into the hall. Her arm throbbed a little where she'd cut herself. She knew this would stop after half an hour or so. It always had before.

The carpet in the hallway was blue-gray and plush. There were no irregularities in the texture of its surface. Her mother always made sure that the carpet, the mirror and the top of the hall table were spotless and perfect. It seemed to calm her mother to clean them. Samantha noticed that if her mother was agitated, she would vacuum or dust or polish a mirror, and it was as though she had a whole different personality when she was finished.

Samantha walked down the carpeted stairs in slow motion, holding the banister firmly and concentrating on each step. She had been feeling light-headed and was afraid of falling.

* * *

Phoebe McIntyre, the student with the highest grades in her school, the student who was rated in the top 1 percent of the country's high-school students based on her SAT scores, and who would certainly graduate with many honors, felt completely stupid.

She got off the phone and thought about what Jessica had told her. More than anything, she wanted to lose weight, to have a small waistline—or any waistline—to have slender thighs, and to feel carefree in her clothes instead of feeling imprisoned by them.

Phoebe thought about her weight all the time, and about wanting to be Daryl's girlfriend: tall, cute Daryl, with his easy, relaxed laugh and the strong muscles in his bare forearms.

She visualized herself slender in a red dress. She was in a room full of tables covered with scrumptious food, and she was saying, "No, thank you," to pastrami and thickly sliced rye bread, to tangy pickles, to chocolate of all kinds, especially dark and bittersweet. Dizzy with the wonder of these images, she pictured donuts covered with powdered sugar and pitchers of cold milk. Suddenly, the sadness spilled over like bright, red ink soaking across soft paper.

She took out her journal and began to write as her orange

poodles, Tom and Nicole, scampered maniacally around at her feet fighting over one of her white socks. She wrote:

Why can't I be like other girls? Why can't I be normal?

WHY? WHY? I have never had a date in my WHOLE LIFE. I'm a good person. I got the highest SAT scores in the country. I recycle. I floss every day. I'm nice to my parents. So what if I have some extra weight on my body? I am sick of living in a world where my body is so important and makes me so miserable. I am sick of living in a FAMILY in which my looks are so important. My mother keeps tellng me that life is not a beauty contest, but my dad seems to believe it IS one. So if life is NOT a beauty contest then what IS it?????? I just want to be normal!!!!!!!

Galvanized by a fresh resolve to change, she headed for the little workout room her parents had installed in the basement. Tom and Nicole scurried after her, jumping against her ankles and each other, rushing to keep up as she resolutely pursued her mission to create a new, improved Phoebe.

* * *

Samantha sat at dinner, moving her food around with her fork. Dinner that night was broiled flounder, peas and little potatoes with parsley on them, all served on plain, white china plates. Occasionally, she pierced a potato with her fork, stalling for time. She knew that if she could prolong her playing-with-the-food routine long enough that, when her mother started nagging, she could make a scene, storm out, and dash upstairs to lock herself in her room where she would be safe from nags, threats and food. She also wanted to take a look at her injured arm, which throbbed with pulsations that had acquired the quality of a sound, a drumbeat.

Finally, Marge Rosen said, "Sam, you haven't eaten a single thing again."

Her mother was plump, but Samantha saw her mother as obese, as a gross, pillowy woman covered with flaccid, puckered flesh. Her mother certainly knew how to stuff herself, observed Samantha, and she poked her nose into everybody's business. She had nagged Samantha's father into giving up vodka and cigars after his heart attack. She was on his case all the time about how he should relax more, but the more her mother pestered him, the more stressed out he got.

She wanted so badly to feel close to her mother. She used to feel held together by her mother. Her mother would hold her when she was small, and Samantha would feel cradled, enfolded in her mother's softness, which yielded to the weight of Samantha's body. Her head could rest on her mother's breast, and Samantha would feel safe. Her mother admired her, adored her then, and Samantha could evaporate into the intoxicating fragrance of her mother's shoulder. Her mother understood her, and the completeness of their bond made Samantha feel immensely strong.

But now her mother was nagging and critical, and instead of feeling protected, Samantha felt imprisoned by her. So much had been lost when Samantha had gotten older, bigger.

"Stop being so nosy!" Samantha said to her mother.

"Samantha, don't talk to your mother that way!" said Nat Rosen, who usually did not participate in these discussions. The shiny bald patches at each edge of his forehead looked oily.

Samantha knew her father disagreed with her mother's dissatisfaction about her, that her father thought Samantha looked just fine. Sometimes he'd point to pictures of thin models in magazines and say, "Samantha, she reminds me of you."

Samantha felt sorry for her father. Her mother insisted he not stay as late at the college where he taught. He had to hurry to fit his meditation into his morning routine, and they all had to whisper and tiptoe around while they were getting ready for school so he could have quiet. *Hah!* thought Samantha. *Hurry up and meditate. That's some joke.*

"Why don't you nag *her* about how much she eats?" said Samantha, referring to Patty, her ten-year-old sister, who had already had second helpings of potatoes and peas, along with two slices of bread. Patty slumped in her chair and looked at her lap, a small lap due to her own plumpness.

"Samantha . . . ," said her father, but Samantha had already stomped out of the room and marched upstairs, where she locked the door and turned on the vacuum cleaner. She vacuumed her room for the fourth time that day. She needed her room to be clean and orderly; otherwise, she might follow her mother's demands and eat. She couldn't explain the connection between the orderliness and the eating, but she felt it, and now the vacuum cleaner's loud whirring also served to drown out the persistent calls of her mother standing at the bottom of the stairs and shouting, "Samantha!"

*   *   *

H ow could you do that to me?" Hannah was saying to Kaneesha. It was Saturday, and the girls were sitting at the Golden Apple Café. They were at a table in front of the shop and the brightness of the morning made Hannah squint.

"Oh, Han," said Kaneesha, with feeling, "I'm so sorry." She hadn't touched her cream-cheese–smeared bagel. "I sideswiped a car on Sunrise Highway and I was so upset, so Tanya called that guy at the body shop. We were so freaked out."

"You didn't call me until almost eleven," Hannah said angrily.

"I'm so sorry," whispered Kaneesha.

Hannah looked at her own plate, empty of everything but a few pieces of toasted crumbs. They sat silently. Hannah's back ached, and her throat felt sore. She loved her friend, but she was so hurt. This letdown felt like a big loss and brought a tight-throated spasm of fear. Having her trusted friends forget all about her felt like her mother getting sick, and losing her breast, and losing her hair, and going to the hospital, and dying. It felt like a disaster, not like missing a movie and a night out. It made her feel like a research station in the Arctic Circle, a small square building surrounded by hundreds of flat miles of snow.

"I'm so hurt," she said finally.

"I'm so sorry," said Kaneesha in the same soft voice. "I'm so sorry I hurt you."

Hannah inhaled deeply and smelled the freshness of the air. "Will the car be all right?" she asked. "Your dad's car?"

"Yes," said Kaneesha, "but it's going to cost me a month's pay."

* * *

Samantha and Lacey got to the locker room at the same time and began to change into their cheerleading uniforms: white leather Keds; green tights; short, white pleated skirts; and white turtleneck sweaters, each with a bright green *MRH* on the front. Maple Ridge High, a school in a suburban community fifty-three miles east of New York City, was proud of its teams, and the girls were thrilled to have the privilege of cheering them to victory.

"What happened to your arm?" asked Lacey, noticing the blue plastic Band-Aid on Samantha's left arm, as she slipped into her skirt.

"Oh, nothing," said Samantha, trying to sound casual. "I just got splattered with oil at the restaurant, is all."

"I hope you're not cutting yourself again," said Lacey, concerned.

Lacey knew that Samantha had cut herself at least twice before. Once the wound on her shoulder had become infected and Samantha had to take antibiotics for ten days. Lacey remembered how unsettling it had been for Sam because the medication had to be taken with food.

"I'm not doing that anymore," Samantha lied, turning away to lace up her Keds.

Samantha hadn't told any of her friends that she had been taking diet pills, the prescription kind, not the drugstore kind that all the girls sampled from time to time. She had found the capsules in her aunt's bureau drawer and had stolen six of them. She had taken some diuretics from her aunt's drawer, also. She was happy that it was so easy to resist eating with the help of the pills, and she had lost two more pounds.

The cheerleading captain bounded onto the field and began to call out the cheers they would be practicing that day. As Samantha walked to take her place in the group, she saw dark spots in front of her eyes. She stopped, blinked, and felt frightened. After a few seconds, the spots disappeared, and she forced herself into the routine with feigned energy.

I'll be all right, she told herself. *Soon I'll be able to go home and I can be with my zebras and my vacuum cleaner. Brian will probably call, and everything will be all right.*

Hannah looked at her watch after biology class and realized that she was too weak to go to volleyball practice. She would surely be dropped if she didn't go, but she couldn't. She knew she would pass out if she went, like that time she was walking downstairs from her room to answer the door and had fallen down the stairs. She had never told her dad or anyone else, except Kaneesha. It really scared her because, although she had only bruised her shoulder, she realized she could have broken her neck. She was afraid of falling in public.

She decided she would make some excuse about why she couldn't go to practice. If they dropped her, awful though that would be, at least her bulimia wouldn't be discovered, which would be far worse.

Feeling calmer, she spent the practice time in the library, where she felt safe from the possibility of bingeing. She needed to study for her biology final. It was important to her to get As; vital that she be special in everything she did.

Secretly, she thought that if she had been a better daughter, if she had helped around the house more, then maybe her mother wouldn't have had to die. Hannah thought of her young mother and sighed. Her mother had given birth to her, she realized, when she was only two years older than Hannah was now. Hannah remembered times when her parents would argue about who was going to take care of her. She remembered feeling confused by this because she felt that her mother loved her, but sometimes it just seemed as though her mother preferred to be alone. She wished she could tell her father the stuff she was feeling, but he seemed so uncomfortable talking with her about her mom.

Hannah knew it didn't make any logical sense to blame herself for her mother's death. She talked to herself about it, saying over and over to herself, *It wasn't my fault; it wasn't my fault.* Her mother wouldn't have listened to her if she told her to eat, that she needed her strength if she was going to fight the cancer that was eating her. *Maybe I should learn to pray,* thought Hannah.

Hannah wondered if her grandmother was at home so she could have a visit with her, which often made Hannah feel better. Her grandmother always told Hannah how she prayed for her. Her grandmother prayed in church and she prayed at home, and sometimes she even called that 800 number on the back of that tiny little magazine, *The Daily Word,* to ask the people there to help her pray for Hannah. Hannah pictured hundreds of pale, seraphic-looking women dressed in wispy, white dresses and answering phones somewhere in the Midwest. They took calls from people like her grandmother who asked them to pray for bulimics and starving Ethiopians. Why did her grandmother think they would pray harder for people who purposely threw up their food than for people who had no food, the seriously food-deprived multitudes?

Hannah would hold her grandmother, and they would rock back and forth, and her grandmother lovingly would whisper Italian words Hannah couldn't understand. Hannah could smell the familiar scents of lavender bath soap, lemony laundry detergent and sometimes, if her grandmother was cooking, garlic.

It was her grandmother who taught Hannah to bake biscotti when Hannah was nine. In summer, her grandmother grew tomatoes and peppers in a small garden on the side of her garage. Milk tasted creamier in her grandmother's house, and the air seemed to have more oxygen in it there.

"I pray you'd let me feed you, cara," her grandmother would say when Hannah refused the chilled green grapes and homemade cannoli.

Hannah was tired. She left the library and walked the eight blocks to her house, which was on a tree-lined street. Shadows deepened as she came into the cool center hallway. She steeled herself when she found her thoughts turning immediately to food, and headed directly to her bedroom.

Sitting on her bed, she untied her black Converse high-tops, partially unlaced them so she could pull them off easily, and sat cross-legged on her bed.

She took a deep breath. "God, please help me," she begged out loud. She took another deep breath and waited, not knowing what she was waiting for.

Samantha was getting hungry. She knew she would have to eat soon. The time after cheerleading practice was the very worst for her. The exercise she was required to do during the practice made her so hungry she felt faint, but she was afraid that she was so hungry that she wouldn't be able to stop eating once she started. She always carried a liter of diet soda with her for times like this. It would bloat her, and she would temporarily forget her hunger.

She had a free period after practice, so she changed back into her plaid skirt and the gray-green sweater that matched her eyes, and went to the cafeteria just to look at the food. Sometimes looking at the food and smelling it would be enough to satisfy her. All the food in the cafeteria disgusted Samantha, anyway. She was starved, but that food made her wince. There was so much of it: mounds and mounds of beef stew covered with brownish-orange yucky sauce; over-cooked pale-green broccoli glistening with gobs of greasy butter; and cottony white bread. Samantha talked to herself about the food this way, to dissuade herself from being tempted to eat it. She told herself how disgusting it was, how the slices of white bread were so white and so square that they looked like packing material, how the little cubes of beef in the stew would make her look as boxy as they were. She told herself that if she ate little cubes of meat, she would have little cubed things sticking out of her legs and arms and belly. She felt safe with apples. They would keep doctors away! Apples and lettuce were the only two foods she trusted now. A month ago, she was able to eat bagels, too, but even they seemed too substantial to Samantha now.

She got an apple and came back to her seat in a distant, less-crowded part of the room. She sliced the apple into six-teen pieces, then she ate it, piece by piece, very, very slowly. She chewed each bite at least fifteen times and took three breaths between each bite.

As she was leaving the cafeteria, she saw Kevin, one of Brian's friends.

"Hey, Sam," said Kevin in his friendly way, his eyes sparkling with playful mischief. "How goes it? You're looking a little thin these days. What's going on? Too much running?" Kevin knew that Sam was on the track team as well as the cheerleading squad.

Even though the way he'd said that she was thin didn't sound complimentary, she was happy he said it. That meant she was thinner than normal; she was special, not ordinary.

"Hey," she said, "you're looking kind of fat." She said it smiling, and he, knowing he wasn't fat, smiled back and waved as he walked toward the table where his friends were laughing at someone's D on the top of an exam paper. Brian was at that table.

A feeling of intense heat rushed up into Samantha's face as her heart thumped.

❊ ❊ ❊

Jessica looked out the kitchen window at the huge spruce tree that grew at the edge of the yard. She'd always thought of this as her tree of blue feathers, so delicate were its silky needles. The tree reminded her of her father, who loved to grow things and care for them. During one summer, when it hadn't rained even once, he'd watered

biking helmet. She saw the meat loaf left over from last night's dinner. Beside it was half a lemon meringue pie covered with plastic wrap. The lemon meringue pie was for tonight's dessert. She took out the meat loaf and sliced off a thick piece. She placed it between two slices of white bread. Then she took it upstairs to her room so that she could eat it in private. She checked her answering machine to see if she had any messages before she started on the sandwich.

She kept hoping in her daydreams that Daryl would have fallen in love with her and called. She sat near him in English class as often as she could and always gave him her most radiant smile. He was so friendly, and had the whitest teeth and gorgeous, wavy, blond hair.

There was a phone message, but it was from her gym teacher, asking her to come to her office the next afternoon to "have a talk." Phoebe knew of just what this "talk" would consist. She was used to talks like this by now. The teacher would ask Phoebe if she had a problem at home. Phoebe would say, "No, why are you asking?" and the teacher would say, "Well, Phoebe, it's clear that you have a problem with eating." Phoebe would then lower her eyes and mutter something about liking sweets a bit too much, maybe, and feeling completely humiliated. The gym teacher would say sternly that it was not good for Phoebe's health for her to be carrying all that extra weight, and Phoebe, ashamed beyond what she could possibly express, would leave the school and go straight to the candy store to comfort herself with Snickers and Dove bars. This was what had happened in school at least once every year for as long as Phoebe could remember.

Phoebe had always been fat, it seemed. The pictures in the large family photo album showed her as a fat baby, a fat child, a fat camper, a fat Girl Scout.

Having a father who was a professional photographer didn't help. He considered every single situation a Kodak moment. Her father was on her case all the time about her weight, and she felt she could never, ever please him. Even if she lost weight, she would never be tall like the models whose statuesque figures he was used to by now. The "tall blond people," she called them. Phoebe's mother didn't even try to protect her from her father's critical remarks. Her mother turned her back and pretended to be absorbed in emptying the dishwasher whenever Phoebe's father began to discuss Phoebe's weight. Phoebe's father was nagging her about getting therapy. Once he'd even threatened to send her away to some rehab somewhere. Now, Phoebe wondered if she shouldn't consider the therapy idea. Her father said he knew of someone she could see. But first she wanted some mayonnaise on her meat-loaf sandwich.

She went downstairs to the kitchen with a feeling of

excited anticipation. She put mayonnaise on one of the slices of bread and put butter on the other. Someone else might think this was an awful approach to meat loaf, which already had a lot of fat, but she loved it this way. She ate the sandwich too quickly, and then ate eleven Oreos, first scraping off the sugary layer. The chocolate parts were her favorite. She chewed and swallowed, and chewed and swallowed, and waited for something in her to open, for that magical unfolding of her thin, glorious self to emerge. While she waited, she washed down the cookies with two glasses of milk. She felt the extra size of her belly pressing on the zipper of her jeans, felt the waistband cutting her middle, so that it left angry red marks in her flesh when she took off her clothes. Even her green Doc Martens felt tight around her ankles.

* * *

Jessica decided to walk home after school to burn more calories. She had to walk fast, though, because her mother, a television actress, had an audition to attend, and Jessica had promised to watch Matthew while her mother went into the city for her 4:30 appointment. Her mother worked very hard at keeping her own figure trim. She needed to work in order to support Jessica and her brother, especially since Jessica's father had died of AIDS. It was while her father was sick that Jessica had begun to starve herself. The thinner and more frail he became, the guiltier Jessica felt about being healthy.

The kids in school were kind to Jessica during this time, but behind her back they said many negative things about her father. He'd been a nurse and had contracted the disease in the course of his work, but there were whispers about his having been gay. Jessica had heard these rumors and tried her best not to let them bother her, but what if they'd been true? Jessica worked hard at not letting herself visit that fear. It bothered her, too, that she had been so angry with her father for being sick, for having a dreadful disease, for dying, for leaving them all. During that time she'd felt as though she'd had no life of her own, as if her whole life belonged to him, to his disease, to his dying.

Jessica walked quickly and, as she walked, she noticed her heart beating very fast. She felt a little queasy, and there was a slight dizziness behind her eyes. She felt chilly, too, even though it was a warm, spring day.

When she got home, she had so much to do that she forgot all about these unsettling feelings. Matthew wanted her to play video games with him. Then she took him up the street to play with his friend while she made his supper. As she prepared macaroni and cheese, his favorite meal, along with brussels sprouts (she thought he was so cute to love brussels sprouts so much, especially when everyone else in their right mind hated them), she had a sudden attack of weakness and found herself falling onto the beige linoleum floor before she could grab the side of the counter. She fell onto her side, her bare thigh resting beside the metal leg of the kitchen table, the leg with the little dent in it from where Matthew had run into it with his orange Tonka truck. When she tried to get up, she noticed the floor was slightly sticky from old apple-juice spills. There were grains of sand in the tiny crevices between each square of linoleum. The linoleum felt cool against her skin. She thought, *Something dizzying is scaring me,* and *The room is breathing but I'm not,* and *I don't want to die.* A black ant crept past her, shiny as patent leather.

Suddenly, Jessica remembered her future. She recalled the prom dress she was tie-dying in shades of red, with swirls of poison green and touches of lavender. She thought of the "Come as a Puppy" party she was planning for Matthew for his seventh birthday. Everyone would have to walk around on all fours and eat their cake and ice cream out of bowls on the floor.

Terrified of losing consciousness, she struggled to stay in touch. Panic was making her heart beat quickly, and she couldn't seem to catch her breath. She could hear her heart pounding and feel her pulse racing. She sensed her blood rushing through her head, roaring through. She was dizzy, too, and there seemed to be colored lights spinning around behind her eyes, as though an ambulance was parked inside her head. Jessica told herself to take it easy, to slow down and breathe deeply. She told herself to keep struggling to stay conscious.

She enjoyed watching her own mind, following it to places it would take her. She liked history, but not the World War II kind. Instead, she was curious about who first had the idea of shaving, of scraping hair off your body; about who figured out that you could eat cashew nuts, even though their skins were highly poisonous.

When she told herself that nothing horrible was happening, she didn't believe it. She told herself that people who don't eat have these moments every now and then, and that everything would be all right, but she didn't believe that, either.

She focused all her attention on each breath. Breathing connected her to the very first breath she'd ever taken, and it would continue uninterrupted until she had exhaled for the last time. It was the same breathing she'd done as an infant, a toddler, a freckle-faced ten-year-old.

In a few minutes, everything wasn't all right. The colored lights behind her eyes were still spinning around, flashing, twirling behind her closed eyelids, a crazy-looking internal light show that terrified her. Her sense of the room was that it was rotating. She was breathing, but shallowly, a mere thread of a breath, a whisper.

* * *

Before Samantha left school, she remembered that she'd gotten a note from the guidance counselor, who had asked to see her. She told herself the meeting was probably going to be about colleges, but she feared that the counselor might ask about her weight.

Mrs. Antonio, a tall woman with gray-streaked hair worn in a long braid, looked carefully at Samantha as Samantha walked to the chair on the other side of the office. She noticed how loosely Samantha's jeans hung around her hips. It seemed almost as though the girl didn't have a body, that her empty clothes had gained the ability to move without being occupied.

"Samantha," she said, "how have you been feeling lately?

I'm asking you this because two of your teachers have remarked to me that you have been, well, uncharacteristically lazy in class."

Samantha looked around at the certificates and diplomas on Mrs. Antonio's wall. Samantha thought, *New York State says she is qualified to do this job. New York State is a big office building that is trying to make me fat, as fat as an office building.*

"You know," Mrs. Antonio continued, "if there is anything you need to talk about, I'd be happy to see you."

Hah! If I talk to her about this, she, with the blessings of New York State, will make me fat, Samantha told herself. *She might even put me into one of those hospitals where you have to wear awful paper gowns that open at the back and have a sugar tube plugged into your arm.*

"There's nothing wrong," said Samantha. "I just feel like I'm coming down with the flu or something."

Why is she singling me out? thought Samantha suspiciously.

"You have lost quite a bit of weight over the last few months, it seems," said Mrs. Antonio.

Samantha said nothing. She looked at her lap and forced herself to breathe evenly. She was pleased, though, and proud. People had noticed her accomplishment, her triumph. She wasn't average. Other people's insides were chaotic, cluttered. She looked at the M&M's on Mrs.

Antonio's desk. Chocolate! In all those ridiculous colors! They didn't even look like food. It was disgusting. *I could never eat that sort of food,* thought Samantha, as she left the guidance counselor's office.

✳ ✳ ✳

After school, Hannah, too, had an appointment with her guidance counselor. They were going to talk about colleges.

Mrs. Lundquist noticed the circles beneath Hannah's eyes and that her thick, wavy, light-brown hair, which had been gloriously silky and shiny at the beginning of the year, was hanging limply around Hannah's pale, oval face. The shape and size of Hannah's body were well concealed behind her baggy, beige carpenter jeans. Mrs. Lundquist had come to know Hannah fairly well in the two years since Hannah's mother had died, and she was well aware of the changes in Hannah.

Before they talked about colleges, the guidance counselor asked Hannah if she thought about her mother often.

Hannah immediately started to cry. Hannah noticed a soft

teddy bear on Mrs. Lundquist's bookshelf. Mrs. Lundquist saw her looking at it and brought it over to her, along with a box of tissues. Hannah took the tissues, but let the teddy bear fall onto the floor.

"So you want to let this bear just lay on the floor?" said the guidance counselor.

"Yes," said Hannah, sniffling.

Mrs. Lundquist picked up the teddy bear and handed it to her.

"I'm too old for teddy bears," sniffed Hannah.

"I'm not," said the guidance counselor.

Oh, thought Hannah, *you want me to play and talk to the teddy bear, is that it? Like in the psychology books? Well, I don't want to.*

"I came here to talk about colleges," said Hannah firmly.

Mrs. Lundquist didn't answer at once. The silence felt suffocating to Hannah, whose own words hung uncomfortably in the space between them. She felt she had to speak. She was afraid that if she did speak, though, the sadness in her heart would make her cry again. She sat quietly and crumpled the tissue, but she needed desperately to talk.

✳ ✳ ✳

Samantha arrived home from her appointment with Mrs. Antonio feeling anxious. To calm herself, she vacuumed her room and thought about Brian, who hadn't called her since they'd broken up. She still thought of him as her boyfriend. She hated the idea of thinking of him as an ex-boyfriend. He had said she was too moody and too skinny. Imagine. Imagine feeling as fat as she did and having someone tell you that you were too skinny.

She put on a Marilyn Manson CD. *What's wrong with people?* wondered Samantha, as she vacuumed the pale-green carpet, making sure to pay extra attention to the part that came closest to the legs of her desk and her bed.

She had to admit, though, that she understood what he meant about the moodiness. The time Brian had to work late at the supermarket, she had blown up at him because it was the anniversary of the day they'd met and she'd wanted to spend the evening with him. Another time, when he was late coming to pick her up, she had really let him have it. He'd been later than planned because he had to take care of his little brother until his father got home. But didn't he love her? Didn't love eclipse all these things? She knew he would forgive her if she called him and apologized.

She turned off the vacuum cleaner and the Marilyn Manson CD and looked around her room. It was spotless.

All of her music, the cassettes, too, were stacked in alphabetical order in their organizers. The clothes in her closet were arranged by color and length. The sweaters were folded on their shelves, and her books were lined up in order of size in their bookcase. Excellent. She was safe.

She was ready to dial Brian's number, hoping he wasn't working that afternoon and that he'd pick up his phone. Sometimes he didn't pick up his phone when he was practicing his guitar.

"Oh, hi, Sam," he said, after the phone had rung nine times. He said it kind of flatly, not with disappointment exactly, but nearly. Then he didn't say anything else. He didn't sound angry, but she felt fear rising within her from her stomach, past her chest and into her throat.

"Hi," she said brightly. "What are you doing?" She was pretending that what had happened between them a few days ago hadn't happened, hoping he would just let it go.

"Did you just come home from work?" asked Samantha, when Brian failed to respond.

"Yes," said Brian, but he didn't get chatty, and he didn't warm up to the conversational tone she had assumed.

"Sam, what do you want?" he asked impatiently.

"I want to know what you're doing," she replied, unable to mask the tone of defensiveness in her voice.

"I'm just hanging around. I have to watch Cody until my

mom comes home from work." Cody was Brian's little brother. He and Samantha used to take him out for pizza after school, and Samantha would pretend that Cody was their own little boy and that they were a happy family.

"Samantha . . . ," said Brian. This scared Samantha because he had never, ever, even once called her by her full name. "I meant what I said. I'm spooked by being with a girl who won't eat. It freaked me out to be around you after a while, when all you would eat was an apple or something, or some lettuce. It would have been okay if you were fat, but you're so skinny. I felt if I hugged you I would hurt you. I think you need some help, Sam," he said, sounding a little warmer now, with concern in his tone.

Samantha didn't know what to say.

"I can't be with you," he continued, "and the cutting, that bothered me, Sam, it really did. You need to have someone look at all the cuts you made on yourself. I got to thinking that if you hated yourself so much, why did I like you?"

"How could you leave me when I need someone so much?" asked Samantha.

Brian said nothing for a few seconds. "Obviously, it wasn't me you needed," he said finally, "because you were just getting worse and worse all the time. I began to wonder if there wasn't something wrong with me, too. I hope you can find a way to get some help, Sam." Then he said good-bye and hung up.

Samantha, terrified and chilled by his words, vacuumed her spotless, dust-free room again. Then she took her tweezers and pierced the flesh of her shoulder at the edge of her collarbone. The pain focused her entirely. She removed the top layer of the skin in a round shape the size of a dime. Her relief was immediate. It was as though all the hurt and confusion had flown out of her. Then she carefully bandaged the wound and thought about the things Brian had said: that she was too skinny and she never ate. But she realized those were the things she was proud of. She didn't think about what he said about cutting herself. It was as though he never said it.

* * *

Hannah waited to get home before she looked at the results of her math exam. When she looked at the page and saw all the red Xs down the left side where Mr. Contrada had indicated the wrong answers, she was horrified. She had gotten a C. She had never gotten less than an

A. She felt so empty, so hungry and scared.

She called Kaneesha, whose machine said, "If you want money, go away. If you want to sell me something, it better be clothes. If you are a friend, let's party soon. If this is Tanya, where's my red tank top? Later. Beep."

She called Douglas, the one boy in school she felt comfortable with. They could talk about anything. His answering machine said, "I'm probably underneath my Camaro, but leave a message for when I'm vertical."

Hannah sighed. She went downstairs to see what was in the refrigerator and found roast beef, some mashed potatoes and half a blueberry pie. She looked in the freezer, where she already knew she'd find vanilla ice cream and cheesecake. In less than half an hour, she ate a roast-beef sandwich, two pieces of pie and half the cheesecake. She frowned as she slipped the first creamy spoonful of ice cream into her mouth. What had looked like caramel swirling through the vanilla was actually the sauce from some General Tso's chicken. Her father had that annoying habit of plunging whatever spoon he had just finished using into the ice cream carton. The taste of the spicy chicken on her tongue—when she had expected the melting, exotic sweetness of creamy vanilla—was gross.

These were small complaints, she admitted, but you could do something about the small complaints. The big complaints—like global warming, which would result in the ending of the world by flooding as a result of snow defrosting somewhere in the north—you could do nothing about. She scraped the residue of the Chinese sauce out of the ice cream and finished the pint.

Jessica was stretched out on the kitchen floor, afraid to even try to get up. When the phone rang, she felt grateful at first, grateful for some company during what she was going through. But then, very quickly, this feeling of gratefulness turned to fear that someone would find her out. She grasped the door of the cabinet under the sink and clung to it while she moved toward the phone, but the answering machine had already intervened. She heard Phoebe's voice say, "Jess, I need to talk. Could you call me back soon?" Then Phoebe hung up.

Jessica felt panic rise within her. She was so confused by her conflicting feelings. She wanted badly to talk to someone, but she was afraid that if she told anyone about how seriously weak she was, someone might do something about it, something medical, something with hospitals. Her mother would be upset. She didn't want to upset her mother. If she herself had to be hospitalized, who would take care of Matthew? How would her mother work? How would they all live? And what if they made her eat in the hospital?

But Phoebe had sounded as though she needed help. She had never heard Phoebe sound so awful. Phoebe needed her as much as Matthew and her mother did.

Jessica valued her relationship with Phoebe. You could always count on Phoebe to come through for you, and, what's more, you could always count on Phoebe to be fatter than you were. It was awful, Jessica knew, to think this way, but it was the truth.

She was feeling a bit better. Not really better, but less bad. Her heartbeat had evened out. The spinning lights behind her eyes had receded. She had broken into a sweat, and felt chilled. She got up slowly, carefully, holding onto the counter for support. She sat on the stool near the kitchen counter and dialed Phoebe's number.

"I got your message," said Jessica, as calmly as she could. She felt reluctant about telling Phoebe she had fallen. "You sounded so upset, Phoeb. What happened?"

"I ate so much stuff just now," said Phoebe. "I can't stand myself anymore, Jess. I'm fat and disgusting, and I can't stop eating. I don't know what to do."

As soon as Jessica heard the need and desperation in Phoebe's voice, she forgot about everything that had just happened to her, the weakness, the falling, the spinning and the rapid heartbeat. It was as though none of it had ever happened. She felt safe, and was so relieved to be placing her full attention on Phoebe and Phoebe's need for her.

"Take it easy," said Jessica soothingly. "It can't be that bad. We all exaggerate so much. What could you have eaten that was that bad?"

Phoebe told her that she had eaten the meat loaf with the mayonnaise and butter, and the Oreos with all the milk. "I feel worthless and hulky and lumpy," cried Phoebe.

"You're not worthless or any of those other things. I love you, Phoeb. We all do."

This was true. Phoebe was very loved. She was so open and friendly, and she didn't give the impression that she was ever hiding anything. Her very fatness was a testament to that. She didn't hide the fact that she overate when she was alone. She couldn't. It showed all over her, and she still had the courage to leave the house and come to school and participate in life.

Jessica could sympathize with Phoebe. She had felt worthless, too. The only difference was that Phoebe was so fat. It was not just baby fat or elementary-school fat or cookies-and-milk fat. This was high-school fat, really serious, almost grown-up fat. This was the kind of fat unfathomable to Jessica. That Phoebe could be fat and still go on with her life fascinated Jessica, and her regard had a tinge of admiration, of mystery, even glamour. She felt close to Phoebe, and awed by her, too.

"I'm a big, lumpy blob," said Phoebe. "What am I going to do?"

Jessica thought about how miserable Phoebe was, compared her own misery to Phoebe's, and decided that Phoebe's misery was worse.

I'm having trouble with my energy right now, that's all, Jessica told herself, *but my clothes fit. I look great. I'm a cheerleader. I'm on the debate team and I'm thin. I'm so lucky.*

"Look," said Jessica, "why don't you come over here right now so you don't have to be alone and we can talk. I'm going to pick up Matthew and I'll be right back. Wait for me if I'm not here. Okay?"

Hannah buttoned and unbuttoned the cuff of her blue plaid shirt. She kept her eyes in her lap as she sat waiting for the guidance counselor to finish her phone call.

When Mrs. Lundquist hung up the phone, turned toward her and said, "Hannah . . . ," Hannah began to cry. It surprised her. All it had taken was hearing her name, her own name, spoken tenderly, and she'd started wailing. She was so ashamed. She had so many unshed lonely tears.

The guidance counselor sat opposite her and waited for her to say something. This kind of silence made Hannah feel awkward in the past, but now she liked it. She felt a kind of excitement, an expectant waiting, a readiness to be heard that made her feel special and calm and ready to open.

She wiped her tears away with the tissue that she had pulled from the flowered box beside her on the desk and looked up at the guidance counselor. "Mrs. Lundquist," she said. She was practicing. She was hearing herself say Mrs. Lundquist's name as she had many times before when she'd practiced this speech at home. The speech always sounded stilted, like someone reading a script written by someone else.

"What is it, Hannah?" said the guidance counselor. She said these simple, ordinary words, Hannah thought, with concern, as though Hannah was very precious, very important, as though she really cared about what was wrong.

Well, thought Hannah, *here goes.* "Mrs. Lundquist," said

Hannah, this time feeling as though her words sounded more natural, "I think I'm a lesbian."

The guidance counselor showed no change of expression and nothing about her body shifted or twitched, which was the reaction Hannah had expected. She had expected shock or alarm or dismay, but no such reaction occurred.

"Well," said the guidance counselor softly, as though talking to a wounded child, "do you want to talk about it?"

"No," said Hannah, "I just wanted to say it, to hear myself say it, to say it to someone."

The guidance counselor was silent so that Hannah could hear the aftermath of her own words. Hannah crumpled the tissues and thought about what she'd said. She was wondering what the guidance counselor really thought.

"How does all this make you feel?" asked Mrs. Lundquist. "What makes you think this about yourself, Hannah?"

"All my friends are always talking about guys and stuff, and I just don't see what's so intriguing about them. I keep thinking about girls. Whatever," said Hannah, as she looked at her denim lap. She felt relief warming her hands and arms. She had been unable to say anything about this to anyone, not even Kaneesha or Tanya or Doug. "I feel pretty scared about this," said Hannah. "I can't stand feeling this different, this alone." She felt afraid of thinking about it. Sometimes she talked to herself to calm herself down, but no amount of talking calmed her about this.

"What's scary about it?" said Mrs. Lundquist.

"Well, isn't it scary to you?" asked Hannah.

"Should it be?"

"Well, it's so, I don't know, so different," answered Hannah, unable to find the words she needed.

"Not that different," said the guidance counselor. "Ten percent of people the world over are homosexual." Hannah hated that word. It sounded so clinical. She hated any word that had the word "sexual" in it.

"I didn't know that percentage stuff," said Hannah.

They were both quiet for a moment. Hannah looked at the pattern in Mrs. Lundquist's slacks, the little threads of lavender in the petals of the flowered print. She shuddered to think of having her father know about her differentness. She wondered what her mother would have thought about it.

"I don't feel comfortable even thinking about my father knowing," said Hannah. "I don't even feel comfortable knowing myself. I feel as though I'm invading my own privacy or something."

"Nobody has to know," said the guidance counselor. She rose and walked to her desk, then shuffled some papers in a drawer. She came back and handed Hannah a booklet entitled *Gender Anxiety*. "Maybe this will help. Maybe it can keep you company a little," suggested Mrs. Lundquist. "Anyway, maybe we can talk a bit to help you feel more comfortable. And thank you for trusting me, Hannah."

"I just feel so lonely about it."

"Absolutely," agreed the guidance counselor. "It feels so lonely to be different. Sometimes differentness feels like a blessing, but sometimes it feels like a curse, too."

"Yes," said Hannah gratefully. She was breathing more deeply now. She exhaled one long breath and settled more comfortably into her chair. She noticed things about the room: the sun streaming in the windows illuminating the dust in the air, the walls painted a muted green, the huge old wooden desk with the jar of ballpoint pens, the white cardigan draped over the back of a chair. She felt as though she had come out of a dark tunnel.

"You must feel different because of your mother's illness and death, too," said Mrs. Lundquist.

"I do," said Hannah, "and I just feel as though I have to try harder than other people do. I don't know. I feel so lonely and so empty."

"People feel empty when they aren't feeling their feelings," said the guidance counselor gently.

Hannah thought about this. She felt like it was a big idea

that she wouldn't be able to take in all at once, and she filed it for later consideration.

"Hannah," said Mrs. Lundquist, "some of your teachers are concerned about your grades. You've been dropped from the volleyball team, I understand, and your phys ed teacher is worried about your low weight."

"Well, I'm not worried about it, so why should she be?" replied Hannah crossly. Hannah felt afraid again. She could feel herself drawing away to that safe, silent, distant place inside herself.

"Why don't we make a date to talk again, Hannah?" asked Mrs. Lundquist, standing up to find her appointment calendar.

"I don't know," answered Hannah. "Let me think about it."

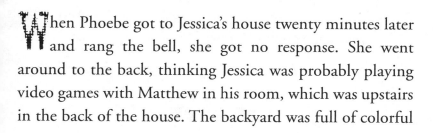

When Phoebe got to Jessica's house twenty minutes later and rang the bell, she got no response. She went around to the back, thinking Jessica was probably playing video games with Matthew in his room, which was upstairs in the back of the house. The backyard was full of colorful plastic toys. The red barbecue grill was rusting near the doghouse, where Aladdin, the sheepdog, was snoozing. Aladdin wagged his tail when he woke and saw Phoebe, who often brought him bones. He came over to her, nuzzling her hand and drooling on her jeans as she squinted through the screen door.

When a minute or two had passed and she'd received no reply, she opened the dusty screen door and went down the cool hallway to the bright kitchen. Jessica was crumpled on the beige linoleum, looking frighteningly pale. Blood pooled on the floor beside her, and Phoebe noticed blood on the edge of the marble countertop. "Oh, God," said Phoebe.

Phoebe had never had to call 911 before, and dialing felt unreal, as though she was watching herself on TV. Her hands were freezing. Heart pounding, episodes of *ER* sped through her mind as she described to the operator what she had found. Her jaw felt painfully tight, her chest weighted down by a cement block. The operator had told her to wait after asking her a series of questions that seemed interminable as Jessica remained on the floor, scarily unmoving.

The piercing shriek of sirens began almost as soon as she hung up.

*　*　*

Stretched out on the floor at the end of her yoga class in black leggings and a white T-shirt, Hannah stared at the white ceiling and enjoyed the warm infusion of energy she felt flowing through her body.

"Inhale," the teacher was saying. "Let the weight of your body melt into the floor. Let go. You don't have to control everything. Relaxation is about yielding."

Hannah, hearing the phrase "the weight of your body," stopped breathing. Every muscle, so carefully stretched for an hour, tensed. As the class came to an end with instructions to relax and let go of the need for control, Hannah's heart raced. Anxiety about her weight, anxiety about her math class, anxiety about her biology final flooding her awareness.

✳ ✳ ✳

The black clogs that Samantha had bought herself on her sixteenth birthday, which had taken her everywhere, stood on the floor at the edge of her night table. Samantha's size-seven feet slipped into these clogs on the morning of her seventeenth birthday. In them, she descended the carpeted stairs. She walked out the front door and into the driveway. There she found her very own used 1993 Mazda Protegé that she would be driving all by herself for the very first time. It was steel gray, an iridescent pewter shade that made Samantha think of the moon, of powerful machinery, of possibility, and of strong masculine force. The sound of the engine springing to life sent a thrill moving through her.

As she put the car in reverse and backed slowly out of the driveway, her wide street, Stonehenge Road, seemed suddenly small, narrow, suffocating, a place from which she needed to escape. Samantha drove the two miles down the wide, leafy avenue, all her senses heightened with the triumph of her new freedom. Making the right turn onto Main Street, she noticed that the jewelry store that had been on the corner for as long as she could remember was going out of business. Two doors further down at the new restaurant called 57 Fireflies, grand-opening banners were waving in the breeze.

She made the left turn that took her to Jenna's white house. The driveway gravel crunched as the Mazda slowed and rolled to a stop at the fence, which surrounded the pool. Jenna was in the pool. Samantha could hardly wait for her to dry off, scrunchee up her hair, and get into the car with her. The fast-beating excitement of her heart made her forget the cutting, and the recent tensions between her parents, and Brian, and how hungry she felt.

Samantha's mother, Marge Rosen, sat in the basement of the Presbyterian church surrounded by unfamiliar faces. She listened to a woman describe how much Al-Anon had changed her life. Marge had come to the meeting at the urging of her hairdresser, who had been going to the meetings for years.

"But I thought Al-Anon was only about people who lived with alcoholism," protested Marge.

"Well, it's not," said Donna, as she blow-dried Marge's new, shorter, layered, light-brown hair. "It's for any kind of behavior you can't control, and you're always telling me how worried you are about Sam."

Marge sat up straighter as the woman in the church basement talked about her son. The woman was shredding a Kleenex as she talked.

"I begged and nagged and criticized, and I preached and manipulated and cried about his drinking and pot use," said the woman. "Finally, I realized I had to take charge. I said to him, 'Either you give up the self-destructive behavior or you can't live here.' I learned in Al-Anon you have to present a consequence," she said to the group. "It worked so well, I can't believe I hadn't tried it sooner."

Marge asked the woman to have coffee with her after the meeting. The woman—about Marge's age with lank, blond hair and pale, watery eyes—said yes.

"I need to know everything you know," said Marge excitedly as they left the church and headed for the Silver Spoon Café across the street.

* * *

Hannah sat in a shaft of sunlight in her bedroom studying for her biology final, but she couldn't remember much of what she was reading. The part about the anatomy of the heart disturbed her. Her mother had actually died of heart failure brought on by undereating, not from her cancer. Reading words like *ventricle* made Hannah feel as though she was back in the fear she had experienced every day when she was little. In addition to the cancer, her mother had heart trouble for a number of years before she died. Every day when Hannah went to school, she wondered if her mother would be alive when she returned home. She was always reluctant to go to school then, often locking herself in the bathroom and refusing to go, because she knew that one day she would go to school and, when she returned home, her mother would be dead. In fact, that was exactly what had happened. Hannah wondered whether her mother would still be alive if she hadn't gone to school that day. Maybe her mother was so sad, so lonely, she'd died of a broken heart. Maybe if Hannah had been home . . .

Hannah couldn't concentrate on hemoglobin. She knew that she needed to study biology, but instead she spent the whole afternoon thinking about her mother's heart.

She tried on her jeans (if they zipped, she was safe) and inspected her stomach in the mirror. It was nearly flat. Her thighs still seemed too large, but she took pleasure in her small waist, which made her forget that her biology final was less than a week away. She needed a perfect grade; without it, she would get a dreaded B for the term.

Food drifted into her thoughts. Should she defrost some shrimp and have them with warm, crusty bread and lots of butter?

* * *

Jessica woke up in a sunny room at Heathbrook Hospital with a needle in her arm. The needle was connected to a tube, which had clear liquid flowing through it into her. She knew she was getting calories pumped into her. She was terrified of the needle, the tube, the calories.

A nurse hovered near her bed, a chubby nurse, with round, apple cheeks. The front of the nurse's uniform strained to stay closed across her ample bosom, and her bulky calves protruded beneath the hem of her skirt.

When Jessica opened her eyes, the nurse said, "Hello. How are you feeling today?"

Jessica's mother had just gone to get a cup of coffee. She had canceled an audition to sit at Jessica's bedside.

Jessica didn't know what the fuss was about. She vaguely remembered that she'd felt light-headed and fallen, hitting her head on the edge of the counter.

Jessica didn't know how long she'd been asleep, or what she thought of as asleep. Now she was entirely awake, jolted into awareness by the prospect of being fed through a tube, by the idea of calories, by the idea of fat being pumped into her. Her vision was a little blurry, but only slightly. She blinked several times to clear her eyes. Her head, though, was splitting. Even her hair hurt.

"I feel like I have fourteen heads and headaches in every one," said Jessica.

The nurse looked at her without saying anything, studying her. "You know what happened, don't you?" she said finally.

"What do you mean?" asked Jessica, shutting her eyes tightly and rubbing her temples.

"Well," said the nurse, sitting down in the green molded-plastic chair beside Jessica's bed, "I want to warn you that you also have a black eye. I don't want you to be too shocked when you finally get up and take a look."

"What happened?" asked Jessica suspiciously. She stopped rubbing her head and regarded the nurse with absorption.

"You don't know?" exclaimed the nurse with surprise.

"No," said Jessica impatiently.

"I'll just go and get the doctor so he can talk to you," said the nurse, as she stood and stepped crisply out of the room.

At first, Jessica felt afraid. Then she felt irritated, as though she'd been scolded.

Shortly, the doctor appeared. He was a tall, beefy, gray-haired man wearing a stethoscope and a serious expression. Jessica didn't like the expression on his face. He looked to her as though he was about to tell her something she was going to hate. She began to feel nauseous.

"Hello, Jessica," he said as he sat in the green molded-plastic chair the nurse had vacated. "We need to talk. I've paged your mom, and she'll be here in a minute or two."

"The nurse wouldn't tell me what happened," said Jessica angrily. She swallowed hard to keep the fear from choking her. Was she going to die? Did she have epilepsy or something? Some sort of vascular disease that was pinching off the blood supply to her brain? What was going on? It made her cranky not to know things. Information gave you control. She needed information. Also, she hated the idea that calories were flowing into her as they sat there, drop by insidious drop. It made her furious that she couldn't even get up to exercise all those calories away.

Jessica's mother came into the room. Adrianne Blaine looked perky in her stretch jeans and a black tank top, her freckled shoulders bare, with a white cardigan draped over them. Seeing that the doctor sat on the chair beside the bed, she perched beside Jessica, causing the mattress to slope toward the heavier side, and making Jessica's head ache even more severely.

The doctor nodded to Jessica's mother, then looked at Jessica. "What happened, we think, is that you were starving, and you passed out from having severely low blood sugar, and your blood pressure was way down. The injury to your head was a result of your falling; that's why it aches so badly and your eye is blackened." He consulted her chart briefly. "It seems your friend, Phoebe McIntyre, found you."

Now Jessica suddenly remembered. She had talked with Phoebe. Phoebe must have come over and found her. How totally embarrassing! Now everyone in school would know.

"So," continued Dr. Moran, "we need to keep an eye on you for a while, stabilize your blood sugar and electrolytes, and let you rest and eat. You're not going to feel like going out dancing any time soon, anyway. Your skull has been fractured. You're lucky it wasn't worse. It could have been your neck or back."

No, thought Jessica, *I'm not lucky at all. I'm stuck in this bed, you're feeding me vile liquids with calories in them, and I can't get up to exercise. I've probably gained five pounds already, and this hospital gown—ugh!*

"How long have I been here, anyway?" asked Jessica warily.

"Two days," replied the doctor, looking at his watch and standing. "You're going to have to eat something now, young lady. I have to see another patient. Excuse me," he said as he left, nodding to Jessica's mother.

He had already had a talk with Adrianne, a talk that had proved frustrating for them both. Dr. Moran maintained that he wanted to keep Jessica in the hospital for another couple of days. Her mother argued that all she had done was crack her skull, and couldn't she just as easily rest at home where her younger brother could keep her company. The doctor was firm and could not be swayed from his decision to keep Jessica for observation.

Jessica turned to her mother. "How do I look?" she asked.

"You look fine, sweetheart," her mother answered. "Just a black eye is all. You'll be fine. What about something to eat?"

The doctor had told her that Jessica must have been starving. Her weight was so low, and her electrolytes were below normal, too, along with her blood pressure.

"But Jess looks great," protested her mother to the doctor. "She's the envy of all her friends."

"She may be the envy of all her friends, but she is too thin and shows no sign of gaining any weight, either," said the doctor resolutely. "I recommend that you get her some therapy, Mrs. Blaine."

"I think she saw someone at the high school," remarked Jessica's mother tentatively. She seemed to remember Jessica telling her that she'd gotten a note from the guidance counselor. She didn't know if Jessica had actually gone for an appointment, though.

Adrianne Blaine smoothed her rust-colored hair away from her face and placed her hands on top of Jessica's. "What would you like to eat, sweetheart?" she asked.

"Oh, Mom, I'm feeling so headachy," protested Jessica. "I couldn't possibly eat anything."

Just as her mother had finished saying, "All right, Jess," the nurse came in with her meal. Roast lamb with mint jelly, mashed sweet potatoes and green beans with almonds.

Do they actually expect me to eat all this? thought Jessica, horrified.

The nurse set the food on Jessica's tray table and left.

* * *

S amantha stood timidly outside the door to Mrs. Antonio's office and hesitated before knocking. It wasn't as though Mrs. Antonio wasn't expecting her. Samantha had called for an appointment. Her mother had basically said she'd have to be hospitalized if she didn't see someone, but that didn't mean she'd have to talk. She was afraid of what might happen, afraid she would be forced to eat. Samantha was wearing her most fattening clothes, therefore: layers of T-shirts and a big workshirt over them all, with baggy chinos from the Gap.

The guidance counselor answered Samantha's knock. Samantha noticed that she was wearing really nice oxfords—they were wing tips—with her own baggy chinos.

Samantha sat down in the brown leather chair. She didn't know what to say.

Mrs. Antonio just sat with Samantha for a few seconds. She noticed how pale and thin Samantha's face looked. She said, "How are you feeling today?"

"I feel fine," lied Sam. She felt tired and afraid, and a little shaky because she hadn't eaten in a day and a half and because her shoulder wound felt as though it was becoming infected. It throbbed sometimes. It had turned an angry shade of red and was sore to the touch. Even though she'd washed and bandaged it like she always did before, she thought maybe the tweezers she'd used to make the cuts hadn't been clean enough, or that the medicine she'd put on hadn't been sufficient.

"I feel fine," insisted Samantha, as though repeating it could make it more true than it was. She wanted to be out shopping with her friend, Jenna. She wanted to be home, safe in her room, vacuuming. She felt panicky.

"You look thinner, Samantha," remarked Mrs. Antonio matter-of-factly. "Have you been eating?"

"Yes," said Sam. "I'm eating."

"What? What did you have to eat?"

"A salad," replied Samantha. Two leaves of lettuce was what Samantha referred to as a salad. She couldn't eat more than this at any one time anymore. She had tried, and she just couldn't do it, couldn't let herself. Eating other foods would be like eating a flashlight or a picture frame. They weren't edible to her anymore.

"What was in the salad, Samantha?" persisted the guidance counselor.

Samantha stalled for time. She looked around Mrs. Antonio's office, trying to locate something to focus on. She arranged her face so that it would seem that she was thinking while Mrs. Antonio waited patiently. "The salad was ten leaves of iceberg lettuce," she said, embellishing the truth, "with pepper sprinkled on it and a little vinegar."

"Ten leaves of lettuce is not a meal," said the guidance counselor.

"Why not?" argued Samantha. She would just tough it out, she decided. She refused to be intimidated. "It's a meal to me," she said. "Anyway, I came here to talk about Brian."

"Tell me about Brian," said the guidance counselor. "Tell me about your relationship with him."

"Brian broke up with me because he said I wasn't fun," said Samantha, settling into another lie.

* * *

Phoebe called Jessica at the hospital and heard Jessica's tired voice say, "Hey, Phoeb, you woke me." It was 10:00 in the morning. Jessica explained that for some reason hospitals woke you early, and by midmorning she was tired again. Her face looked as pale as the swirls of gray in her paisley silk robe.

"How are you, Jess?" Phoebe asked anxiously.

"Pretty awful," replied Jessica. "They aren't going to let me out of here any time soon. They want to keep an eye on me." She didn't say anything about eating.

"How are you doing?" she asked Phoebe, affecting a bright tone. "Thanks for picking me up off the floor, by the way."

"I'm eating everything in sight," sighed Phoebe, not wanting to talk about that fateful day. "I can't seem to stop."

Daryl had spoken to Phoebe that day. He had asked her how Jessica was doing. The students at Heathbrook High had learned of Phoebe's "rescue," and Phoebe was enjoying a certain celebrity because of it. She knew very well that it was no more heroic than picking up anything else that had fallen on the floor, but the whole episode had developed a certain mystique, and Phoebe was in the spotlight. Phoebe liked the spotlight, but she wished she had a waistline so she could enjoy it more.

Phoebe was growing fatter. She had noticed that her

clothes were fitting more snugly, even her pleated skirt, even her shoes. Her cowboy boots no longer slipped over her calves, and, worst of all, she had needed to get a new, larger-sized bra.

Daryl had smiled at her so genuinely, though. He'd asked about Jess, and then he'd asked her about herself, about what she had planned for the summer. She told him she was going to work in her father's photography studio. Phoebe couldn't stop thinking about his face, his beautiful strong arms, the way his hair curled around his collar in back.

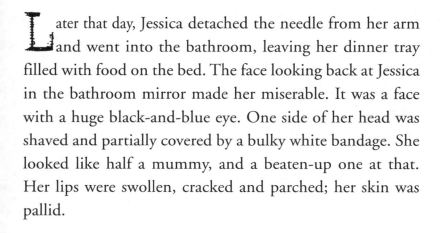

Later that day, Jessica detached the needle from her arm and went into the bathroom, leaving her dinner tray filled with food on the bed. The face looking back at Jessica in the bathroom mirror made her miserable. It was a face with a huge black-and-blue eye. One side of her head was shaved and partially covered by a bulky white bandage. She looked like half a mummy, and a beaten-up one at that. Her lips were swollen, cracked and parched; her skin was pallid.

To top it all off, she was hungry. Her head was pounding and her heart was, too. She was starving even though the liquid calories had been dripping and dripping into her. She couldn't, however, let herself eat. If she let herself eat, she would disappear. Her identity would dissolve into food. She wouldn't allow herself to look this awful and be fat, too. She would rather die than have that happen.

She made her way carefully back to the bed and took the plate with the lamb on it into the bathroom. There, she cut up the lamb into little pieces and scraped them off the plate and into the toilet. She flushed it and then took the green beans and dropped them in as well. The pat of butter went in last. The roll she placed in the drawer on the side of her bed. She was comforted knowing that the roll was in there. She wouldn't eat it, of course. It was just going to keep her company.

She took up her sketch pad and selected some colored pencils from the big box her brother, Matthew, had brought for her. Her mother had brought her a Discman, and she decided to listen to *The Allman Brothers Band at Fillmore East*. As she began to design a new nurse's uniform, all thoughts of food, fat and fear melted away into the miniskirted, white cotton dress she thought would look fabulous on the slim night nurse who had such good legs.

Dr. Moran came into her room and found her sketching.

"Jessica, we have to talk about your problem," he said.

Jessica turned to look at him. "What?" she said, pulling off her earphones.

"We have to talk about your problem," he repeated. "You mean to tell me you're here with a bruised face and a cracked skull, which you got because you were starving yourself, and you don't think you have a problem?"

"No," she said simply.

"Well," said Dr. Moran, crossing his arms in front of his chest, "I've talked to your mother about whether she wants you in the hospital, and she says she wants you home. She says you can take care of the problem yourself, and that there is no point in admitting you to an eating-disorder unit if you don't want to be there. So, as soon as you're strong enough, I'm going to discharge you. But, meanwhile, you must eat if you want to go home. The nurse will feed you to make sure that you do eat."

Jessica knew she was cornered, that if she still refused to eat they'd put a Hyper-Al tube into her. She had heard about that from the nurse. They would make a little hole in the hollow between her collarbones and feed her thousands of calories a day through a tube. She pictured lumps of food flowing through the tube directly into her throat and down to her thighs and stomach. She knew she could get away with eating less than that if she sat with the nurse

and let herself be monitored as she ate. She would eat two
bites of each thing on the obnoxious tray, and then they
would leave her alone. Then, when she got home, she
could diet and exercise all the weight off again. She would
fool them. *I am still in charge of my body, and I will stay in
charge,* she thought as the nurse came into her room.

Hannah was just finishing her biology final. She looked
up and saw Arlette Weiss, the new girl in the neighborhood, standing at the front of the room asking their
teacher a question. Arlette's black hair gleamed in a shining
cap around her face. Her long bangs were cut straight
across. There was something beautiful about Arlette's arms,
Hannah thought, something elegant about their length and
the curves of her shoulders. She wore a lime-green T-shirt
with capped sleeves and faded black jeans that were tight
around her ankles. Her sandals were strappy and brown,
and Hannah could see bright-red toenails. She had seen
Arlette in the locker room, the way her small breasts turned
up like her nose did, with a kind of defiance.

When she got home, Hannah did her usual five-mile jog, promising to herself all the while that she would devote herself to her studies in the afternoon. With her heart beating alarmingly fast after jogging, she took off her damp sweat-clothes and took a shower. She was pleased with how bony she was looking. As she wrapped herself in the comfortingly thick, blue, terry-cloth robe, she noticed that her ribs showed through the thin flesh of her chest.

While she was about to dry her hair, she spread her books on her desk. She opened the history text and propped it against a vase of daisies that her father had left for her. Then she decided that she needed a glass of iced tea, so she went downstairs to get it.

The moment she opened the freezer to get the ice and saw the container of chocolate-fudge ice cream, she knew she was going to eat it, all of it. Still wrapped in her robe with her wet hair hanging about her face, she ate what remained of the ice cream, savoring the chunks of fudgy chocolate as they melted on her tongue. Then she found pretzels, cookies, taco chips and salsa, and Swiss cheese, along with ham, mustard and rye bread.

She ate while staring out the window at the swing set that belonged to the little girl with the mother who was perfectly healthy, the mother who never had to be hospitalized and always appeared on open-school days with the other mothers. The little girl who had pink socks that exactly matched her pink shorts. Hannah hated her.

Kaneesha had made Hannah promise that if she got into one of those eating things she'd call her first, but Hannah couldn't stop. She ate a box of chocolate-covered graham crackers. The sweetness of the cookies seemed to make her crave salt, so she sat at the kitchen table with an icy glass of Diet Coke and ate a box of thick pretzels covered with crunchy salt and dipped in mustard. She thought about how funny it was that she could never let herself drink anything but Diet Coke. She ate the taco chips with salsa, staring at the TV and made a note to remember to replace everything she'd eaten so that her father would not notice that she'd eaten an entire loaf of bread and half a pound of butter and the whole jar of peanut butter right off the spoon. Her experience, she thought, gave the phrase "home alone" a whole new meaning.

By the time she had vomited as much as her aching throat would allow, she went back upstairs, drained, exhausted, starved. She decided to get dressed and go to the store to replace all the food so that she wouldn't have to face her books.

When she got back home, she sat in front of her history books and couldn't concentrate because she felt so hungry. She went downstairs again and ate all the food she had replaced, plus the donuts she had gotten on sale, along with some frozen yogurt in her favorite caramel-and-fudge–swirl flavor, which she hoped would soothe her terribly sore throat.

When the phone rang as she was finishing up the last spoonful of yogurt, she didn't answer it. She knew she would sound hoarse if she spoke. She didn't want to speak with anyone, and she still hadn't studied at all.

* * *

Phoebe visited Jessica on a breezy, warm day. She wore an extra-large T-shirt and red cotton leggings. She had lost about two pounds after working very hard at an exercise routine, but her eating habits had not changed. No matter what she did, she was not able to get a grip on the food, as Jessica used to tell her to do.

Jessica looked horrible.

"Hi," enthused Phoebe, with false cheer. "You look . . . hmm . . . comfortable," was all she could think of to say.

Half of Jessica's head was fuzzy. The half of her face that was bruised had turned from black-and-blue to red, green and a sick-looking shade of yellow around her eye. The bandage looked like a crooked hat.

"I'm glad you came," said Jessica. She really was glad to see Phoebe. It made her feel as though her life was almost normal again, and that everything was going to be all right, and would soon go back to the way it had been.

She felt herself getting stronger. She was eating now. Two bites of toast, two bites of scrambled eggs in the morning. Two bites each of chicken and potatoes and peas at lunch. Two bites of meat and two bites of string beans in the evening. The nurse was not at all satisfied that this comprised eating. She would always urge Jessica to eat one more bite of something, but Jessica was resolute. "I've eaten enough. It hurts when I chew. It hurts my head, and I want to go to sleep now," she'd say. The roll she had placed in the drawer of her bedside table had gotten moldy and greenish. She was surprised no one had discovered it there. They were always poking and prodding her with thermometers and needles and little flashlights.

She couldn't wait to get home. She had it all planned. She would get a variety of pretty scarves and wrap her head. She would make herself thinner again by exercising for three hours every day, to take her mind off her black eye. She was sure she must have gained about twelve pounds by now.

"Do I look fat?" Jessica asked her friend anxiously.

Phoebe swallowed hard. Jessica looked completely emaciated. She looked like she was dying of AIDS. It was hard for her not to think of Jessica as crazy, as deluded.

"No," said Phoebe emphatically, "you don't look fat at all. You just look kind of . . . colorful."

To her friend's surprise, Jessica laughed. Phoebe was sweet, but Jessica didn't take Phoebe's assessment of her size seriously. After all, how would Phoebe know what fat looked like? She was able to live with herself.

Phoebe laughed, too, delighted with herself for having made this spontaneously funny remark, referring of course to Jessica's bruised face.

Jessica didn't say, "I feel ashamed that I haven't admitted that I fell down in the first place because I'd been starving myself," but both girls knew the truth, and Phoebe just sat there, amazed that no one was talking about what was really going on.

Phoebe, however, wasn't talking about what was really going on, either. She was too ashamed of herself. She was too ashamed that she had, in spite of her most valiant efforts, been unable to change her habit of overeating in any way, not even being able to make better choices when the urge to eat overcame her. She envied Jessica. Now *she* was becoming deranged.

* * *

The white leather-covered book said *Phoebe McIntyre's Journal* across the front in red italic letters. Phoebe thought that maybe talking to this book every day might help her sort her thoughts out. It was something she'd seen on *Oprah*.

Phoebe wrote:

My father is driving me crazy, and my mother isn't helping out. She doesn't defend me when he says how fat I am and how he wants me to get my chin operated on. He says I have a too-small chin, that it recedes. I never thought there was anything wrong with my chin. I feel so horrible when he talks to me like that, like I'm nothing, a nobody. I just want to slink away, never to be heard from again. I want to become a missing person, or at least a very skinny, almost invisible person. Not like Jess, because she's too grossly emaciated now and she looks kind of scary.

I just want to die sometimes, especially when Daryl talks to me, which he does

every day now, and I don't understand why.
I don't know what he wants from me. He
always asks me about Jess. He always
smiles and says, "Hey, Phoeb." I never
thought I could have a boy like that take
me seriously or even talk to me. How could
he not know how hopeless it all is for me?

I wish my father would understand. I
wish he could love me and tell me how wonderful I am. Maybe I should try those
Dexatrim things.

Phoebe spent Saturday working at her father's photography studio. She made neat coils out of the electric wires and surveyed the scene. Phoebe was proud of her father's success. Michael McIntyre Studios, Inc., was one of the most well-known commercial photography businesses in New York City. Its files were filled with the names and photographs of the most beautiful people in the world—supermodels, rock stars, athletes, movie stars—but Phoebe felt she—his own daughter—was a disappointment to her father.

Phoebe's mother, Molly, didn't seem to care one way or another. At least she never said anything to Phoebe about Phoebe's weight. Phoebe thought about her mother as she filed away some pictures of young ballerinas. Her mother had her own problems now, taking care of Phoebe's grandparents, who were both ill.

Michael McIntyre was studying a long-legged, dark-haired model in red leotards, who was standing on her head. Audrey, the model, was looking at her father flirtatiously, Phoebe noticed. The model moistened her red lips with her tongue.

"Sweetheart, sweetheart," he said to the model, "this is yoga we're supposed to be doing. Why the red lipstick? Lose the lipstick! Could someone come over here please and make the lipstick disappear?"

Three assistants sprang instantly into action.

"And do something about the hair, too," he added, taking off his glasses and rubbing the back of his hand across his eyes. A hairdresser, a stylist and a makeup artist fussed around Audrey, who still stood expertly balanced on her head.

Phoebe wished she could stand on her head. She envied the model's lean body and decided that when she got home she'd go to bed and refuse to get out of it until she'd lost at least fifty pounds.

Looking at his watch, Phoebe's father walked to the corner of the enormous studio. He looked at Audrey in her red leotards, with her glossy mane of chestnut hair, and unconsciously compared her to Phoebe. At five feet, three inches tall, Phoebe would never achieve that statuesque magnificence, but she could, he thought, do something with herself. She could lose weight. He sipped a glass of carrot and celery juice that his assistant, Martha, had prepared for him.

"What do you think, Martha? Should I send Phoebe to a fat camp?"

"Hmm . . . I don't know," answered Martha as she wiped the white marble counter. She struggled to find a tactful way to tell her employer that she thought Phoebe should figure things out for herself, that fat camp would humiliate Phoebe.

Phoebe finished her filing and came across the huge room in time to see Audrey place herself on her head once again. She'd watched Audrey with her father on many occasions, and noticed that she flirted with him quite aggressively. She wondered if her father ever flirted back.

"Sweetheart," said her father to Audrey, when she was properly positioned on her head and he had checked to make sure that the light was falling on her just right, "could you try to look less sexy? This is yoga."

✻ ✻ ✻

Samantha sat in Mrs. Antonio's office thinking about zebras. She'd read an article on her computer that said that baby zebras memorize their mothers' striping patterns. She wondered what would happen to the baby zebra if it memorized the wrong stripes. Would the baby zebra's mother come looking for it, or would the baby be lost? Samantha thought about her mother. She felt as though she'd memorized the wrong mother.

This time, Mrs. Antonio didn't speak first. She sat there with her hands folded in her lap and regarded Samantha undemandingly.

Samantha felt shy and afraid. "I don't really want to be here," she heard herself say, as though from a great distance. Time seemed to speed up inside her, in her chest, in her forehead, in her throat, and to stand still in the room around her.

"You don't have to talk if you don't want to," said Mrs. Antonio.

"Can we just sit here for a while?" asked Samantha timidly.

It was the first time the guidance counselor had heard the voice of Samantha the little girl in need.

"Of course," replied Mrs. Antonio.

Five minutes of sitting without talking made Samantha feel safer. Now she would talk, but she didn't know where to start.

As though reading her mind, Mrs. Antonio said, "Tell me about your mother, Samantha."

"My mother's a worrier," Samantha said, relieved that the guidance counselor hadn't mentioned her weight. "My father had a heart attack, and she treats him like he's going to break. It's so annoying. I mean, I know about her childhood and whatever, and that her father was a gambler and all that, but it's so boring to have her worrying and nagging all the time." Samantha wasn't saying what she meant, but she didn't know what she meant. At the same time that she hated her mother, she wanted to feel connected to her.

"My father's the quiet type," Samantha continued. "He doesn't seem to have any friends or anything. He's sort of moody. He doesn't hang around with the guys or play golf. He likes to be by himself, and he spends a lot of time in the basement, refinishing things or something. I don't really know what he does down there. Neither does my mom, really. Maybe he's avoiding my mom. He seems more interested in me than in my mother, though. At least he talks to me sometimes. I hardly ever see him talk to my mother, unless they're arguing. If I were my mother, I think I'd be jealous of me."

Samantha couldn't believe she'd done this much talking or that she felt all the things she did feel about her parents.

✳ ✳ ✳

Jessica spent six days in the hospital, eating two bites of each food on her tray, and Jessica's mother felt that Jessica had been in the hospital long enough. She really didn't think Jessica was so sick that she needed a hospital. Jessica was, she said, just run down, and being at home would do her good.

Jessica was discharged. The first thing she did when she got home was cut her hair into a short, punk-looking shape. Then she dyed it orange. She wore purple eye shadow on both eyes for a while to balance the bruises. She wore large, black T-shirts she had cut the necks out of to disguise what she thought of as her extra fat. All in all, her appearance was very admired by everyone at her school. Some of the girls in her grade even started copying her look. She exercised furiously and ate nothing for the first week, and lost all the weight she had gained.

At that point, she made herself a series of outfits out of a shiny, black, synthetic fabric. Each outfit looked vaguely like a wetsuit. She carried a purse she had made out of an oven mitt shaped like a fish, to which she'd affixed sequins.

The day she'd arrived home from the hospital, Matthew had said, "Jess, I need you! Mom was terrible while you were gone. She was a big, mean monster."

Phoebe looked at herself in her bedroom mirror. She not only felt like a disgusting blob, she looked like one. *How can I go on like this?* she wondered. She couldn't bear when her father talked about sending her away to Duke University, where she would have to subsist on a diet of rice and fruit or something. It was agonizing for her to face him each night at dinner, as though she didn't deserve to eat dinner, didn't deserve to eat anything, didn't deserve to take up space, to live.

Her father worked all day long with skinny models, and she knew he would prefer that she looked like one of them. She knew he was embarrassed to introduce her to the beautiful people at Christmas parties at his studio or his dinner parties at their house. They were the faces that appeared in all the magazines. The Ralph Lauren model had been to their house in the Hamptons, and tomorrow the Cover Girl model was coming. One of the Virginia Slims women was a family friend, as well; they all had to go to her wedding. That model from the Calvin Klein commercials had come skiing with them last winter.

Phoebe's mother never defended her against her father's criticisms, which made her furious. Her mother prepared healthful, low-fat meals for the family because her father insisted on it and because her mother, who had been a model herself, liked to keep herself slim. Phoebe would eat those low-fat meals, and then, when she was back in her own room, would feast on the food she had hidden there in her knapsack, in her shoes, in her pockets. The awful thing was that now she really wanted to do something about her weight, but didn't want to give her father the satisfaction of doing anything about it, even if she could resist the icing on the donuts.

* * *

Hannah and Arlette sat beside each other on the bus on the way to school, talking about their Spanish teacher.

Arlette, closing her eyes in feigned ecstasy, said, "Isn't he a complete hunk? He's so Puerto Rican," as though his very nationality held some irresistible mystique.

Hannah had to admit that Mr. Garcia was quite charismatic, with his dark flashing eyes and playful nature, but she was disappointed that Arlette wasn't equally distracted by their English teacher, Ms. Cahill, whom Hannah found fascinating.

This was the day Hannah would find out her grade on the biology final. When Hannah walked into the biology lab, her teacher asked to see her after class. *This isn't a good sign,* thought Hannah as she sat down and watched the teacher hand the other students their test papers with their grades scrawled across the top in red. The teacher said a few things about some of the harder questions which so many of the students had missed. Hannah still hadn't gotten her exam back when the bell signaling the end of the period rang.

She went to the front of the room as the rest of the class was filing out. She was starving and had a pounding headache. Her eyes burned. Her hands felt very cold, and her mouth tasted dry and metallic.

Her teacher asked her to sit down. "Hannah, is there anything wrong?" asked Mrs. Asher.

"Uh, no," Hannah answered reflectively. "Why do you ask?"

"Because you failed the biology final," replied the teacher. "This is so unusual for you that I thought there must be some trouble at home or something. Is there?"

"No," said Hannah, shifting in her seat. She didn't know what to say. She looked at her lap and fidgeted with the edge of her sleeve. "I don't know," she said finally, not looking up.

"Well, I suggest that you go and see Mrs. Lundquist," said the teacher, "and, if you want to, you can take the exam over again. Would you like that?"

Hannah was so grateful about being able to take the exam over that she nearly jumped up and hugged the teacher. "I'd appreciate that a lot," she said quietly, "but I've already been to see Mrs. Lundquist."

"Well, I think you might want to see her again," said the teacher softly.

✳ ✳ ✳

Jessica and her mother stood together at the kitchen counter. Jessica studied her mother. Thirty-six years, thought Jessica, had not been kind. Other girls' mothers looked younger by far than Adrianne, though they were her age. Adrianne had smoked cigarettes and pot, used cocaine, and lost a lot of sleep in the process, probably years and years of sleep if you added it all up. *And,* Jessica decided, *it shows.* Her mother was still auditioning for those typical American-housewife roles in commercials; the ones where a young mother is doing laundry or serving something microwaved to her family, but she wasn't getting those roles any more. Her hair lacked luster, and she seemed worn out. Makeup helped a bit. That was the one thing Jessica and her mother enjoyed doing together, making themselves up and trying on new lipsticks and clothes.

"What do you think of these new earrings?" asked Adrianne.

"They're cool," said Jessica, admiring the silvery angels that dangled from Adrianne's earlobes.

Adrianne Blaine was taller than her daughter, with a slim figure and long legs, of which she was very proud. She showed them off by wearing short skirts and high-heeled sandals. She tore up some lettuce while Jessica mixed a dressing of yogurt, mustard and apple-cider vinegar.

Matthew was sitting at the kitchen table, painting a

picture of Darth Vader in space with a set of watercolors Jessica had brought him. After a while, he went to watch TV in the living room.

"Mom," said Jessica, wiping the counter with a paper towel, "sometimes I feel you don't really care about me, about my life."

Her mother looked up, still holding pieces of lettuce. Her face held amazement and sadness. "Oh, Jess," she said, with lament in her voice. She wiped her hands on a paper towel and moved toward Jessica. "How can you say that? I love you so much. You're the best thing about me." She took Jessica into her arms and hugged her tightly.

Jessica held herself rigidly in her mother's embrace. She felt she couldn't surrender to her mother, couldn't trust her. She remembered the time she had first had her period. Her mother hadn't asked her if it had hurt or how she felt when she realized that her clothes had been stained with blood right there in gym. She'd longed for her father then, because he always seemed to know what to say to her, what to do for her.

She remembered last year when her mother had a new boyfriend. The new boyfriend didn't have any interest in Jessica personally. He never asked her questions about herself or her interests. Her mother had stayed at his house overnight one Saturday when she'd told Jessica she'd be home by 11:00. She didn't come home until 9:00 the next morning, and didn't even call to tell Jessica where she was. Jessica thought she might be dead. She'd even wished her mother had been dead, she'd been so angry.

Her mother held her and rocked her, and Jessica's body stiffened even more.

"I know you love me, Mom. You just don't know how to take care of me. There's a difference."

❊ ❊ ❊

The next time Mrs. Antonio saw Samantha she was wearing layers again: a green-and-white–striped T-shirt, and over it a plaid shirt in shades of green and gray, which brought out the color of her eyes. Far too many layers for such a warm spring day. Her jeans were soft and faded, and Mrs. Antonio could see Samantha's prominent knee bones and the sharp lines of her narrow, too-slender thighs, which Samantha considered fat.

"Samantha," said the guidance counselor, "are any of your friends having problems with food?"

Samantha remained silent and looked at her feet, wiggling her toes in her black clogs, extending her legs to look at her ankles. Then she looked at her lap, where her hands, small and childlike, were folded like tools neatly put away on a workbench.

"Why do you care?" asked Samantha at last.

"I was just wondering if you had anyone to talk to about your eating," said Mrs. Antonio.

Samantha was looking at the floor, at her feet in their clogs. "What's the difference if I talk about something or not? What good can talking do, anyway? All my mother does is nag, nag, nag, and that is a pain in the neck, and it doesn't help. One friend I have, Alexa, is fat, anyway. What could I say to her?"

"Do you have any other friends?"

"I have Jenna. And Lacey," said Samantha. "She's cool."

"Talking is different from nagging," said the guidance counselor, "and talking can do a lot of good, Samantha."

"Why?" said Samantha, with a stubborn, pouty tone.

"I don't know," admitted the guidance counselor. "I don't know if anyone really knows why talking helps people, but most people agree that it does help. There's the ventilating part, just letting off steam, getting things off your chest. It's as though you're too full of something and you need to get rid of some of it so you don't feel like bursting."

Samantha looked irritated. "What I'm too full of some-times is emptiness," she said. "Would I feel less empty if I talked?"

"Yes," said the guidance counselor. "And then there's the ability when you talk," she continued, "to find out what you're feeling on the inside instead of living life as though your appearance is the only thing you have."

"It *is* the only thing I have," asserted Samantha, but she had to admit that what she was hearing seemed to make sense.

The guidance counselor continued, "Unless you know what your habitual feeling patterns are, the only feelings you will ever have, Samantha, are fearful ones. You will feel afraid most of the time, fearful that some undiscovered sector of your being will spring out and startle you."

"Well, I have you to talk to if I want to talk," said Samantha, and then she quickly added, "which I don't."

"Samantha," continued Mrs. Antonio, "I know you don't trust me. I know it's hard for you to be here, and I know you're as afraid of changing as you are of not changing. I know you hate yourself, too, and that somehow cutting yourself makes you hate yourself and your life less. I know you feel nagged at home, and misunderstood by your mother, and by Brian, too."

Samantha said nothing, but everything she was hearing was absolutely true. She felt if she stayed silent now she would be safe from having to change in any way that might scare her. She felt time as a luminous curtain that hung shimmering around them, separating them both from some other reality where things moved and changed and scared you.

Jessica sat in a lawn chair turning the pages of *Allure* magazine, and waited for the charcoal to get hot enough to make Matthew's dinner of barbecued pork chops and grilled vegetables. She marveled at how odd it was for a six-year-old boy to like vegetables so much.

Matthew is great, she thought as she looked at him. His curly hair reminded her of her father's, and so did the pattern it made at the nape of his neck. She thought of her father with longing and loss. He'd always smelled of sterile gauze and antiseptic soap, and she felt safe when she was with him. She felt that same sort of safety when she was with Matthew. She was calmer than she felt with anyone else in the world, almost as peaceful as she used to feel with her father.

Skylar Blaine had been a nurse through and through, taking care of them all in such a way that Jessica felt that, no matter what happened to them, everything would turn out all right.

She didn't have the same faith in her mother, the same feeling of being protected. Her mother couldn't even decide what to wear, and she dated jerks, in Jessica's opinion. How could she be trusted to make important decisions for their family?

Matthew was sitting on the grass beside her chair, going through his marble collection. She loved the way he could concentrate on things, and how, when he got focused like that, he became very quiet and his gray eyes developed an intensity that made him seem much older.

"Jess," he said, looking up at her, "where do marbles come from, anyway?"

"I think they come from different places in the world," said Jessica with uncertainty. "I'll tell you what. Let's go look marbles up on my computer later."

"Did you cut up the vegetables for dinner yet?" he asked.

"No," she said. "What do you want?"

"I want eggplant and onions and tomatoes and red peppers."

"Okay, champ," said Jessica, rising slowly out of the lawn chair and tousling his hair. She stretched her arms and neck. She felt a little dizzy for a minute when she first stood up, but she was getting used to that. She would wait for it to pass and then continue on about her business.

"I don't want those green peppers, though. Yuck!" said Matthew. "They taste like shampoo."

"Have you tasted any shampoo lately?" asked Jessica,

heading into the house with Matthew trailing behind her.

"Sure, all the time. When I wash my hair, the shampoo trickles into my mouth. It's so yucky."

Jessica's own hair was growing back, and she had cut it in a boyish, gamine style. She liked her new look, which many of the girls in school were copying. Her bruises had gone away and her eyes looked larger with her shorter hair.

"Jess," said Matthew, sitting down at the table to drink some apple juice, "I really missed you when you were in the hospital all those days. I was afraid you'd die like Daddy did when he was in that place."

Jessica came over and sat down next to him. "Come here," she said, pulling him onto her lap. He was heavy, and she strained to pull him up. They had a hug, rocking back and forth.

When Matthew had climbed back onto his own chair, Jessica looked at his small hands, the smooth skin of his arms and the pale down on them, and thought again of her father. He had been a small man, very blond, very gentle and soft-spoken, with a way of doing everything slowly which soothed her. Rage at her mother sprang up suddenly in her chest. How could her mother have cheated on a man like that?

Jessica had been in eighth grade and had walked downtown after school. She'd walked the two blocks from school to the drugstore to get the latest issue of *Seventeen* magazine. Her mother had had an audition in the City that day. Her father was at the hospital working. He'd been an operating-room nurse and was working a long shift.

After Jessica had gotten the magazine, she was crossing the street to head back to school to catch her bus. Suddenly, she saw a woman whose head, at least from the back, looked just like her mother's. The auburn hair was in a French braid with a little, brushy ponytail at the bottom, tied with a green ribbon. Jessica had done her mother's hair for her that morning the same way. The woman was in an unfamiliar car, in the passenger seat, which confused Jessica. The woman was locked in an embrace with a tan, muscular man in a blue T-shirt. As Jessica reached the other side of the street, the couple was pulling away from one another, and Jessica, having a new angle from which to survey the scene, realized that this woman was, in fact, her mother. There she was, in full view of the entire neighborhood. How could her mother have done a thing like that? Jessica felt a cold, queasy feeling in her stomach.

It was the next day that her father had told them he had AIDS, that he might be looking sick, losing weight, but that they shouldn't worry, that he was going to be getting the very best medical care at the hospital.

"Let's put those pork chops on the grill, Matty," said

Jessica. "We'll do the vegetables afterwards. They don't take as long to cook."

"I'm glad you came home, Jess," said Matthew, hugging her hips. "I'm glad you didn't die. I don't know what I'd do if you died. I wouldn't want to live either."

"Oh, Matty, don't talk about things like that. I'm here; I'm fine," she said.

* * *

Phoebe's grade on her biology final had been an A-, and Phoebe was glad. Biology was not her strongest subject. She hated the names of inside parts of the body. The word *vagina* made her feel creepy. But she had studied hard.

When she got home from school, she forced herself to walk on the StairMaster for forty-five minutes, which was hard. She checked the monitor often to see how many calories she was burning. She noticed that it took a long time to burn two hundred calories, but only a few seconds to eat them.

Her mother was in the kitchen getting dinner ready when Phoebe came in from the workout room. It had a treadmill and a StairMaster and an entire set of weight-lifting machinery with the word *Cybex* printed on it. They were all bright yellow, and Phoebe liked the look of them. There was a TV in there, too, and a good sound system.

"You're looking fit," said her mother, obviously pleased with her daughter's flushed face.

"I feel tired," said Phoebe.

"Well, we're having dinner soon," said her mother. "Grilled flounder with some tomatoes, broccoli and rice."

Phoebe knew her dad would be pleased with that simple menu, but Phoebe enjoyed richer foods: leg of lamb with lots of garlic in it, mashed potatoes with plenty of butter, and glazed carrots. Crusty bread would make it even better, she thought, as she went up to her room.

She was starved. She opened the door of her closet and took out her blue windbreaker. She reached into the roomy pocket and extracted a cellophane-wrapped, chocolate-covered donut and two Chunkys. She locked her door, sat on the bed, and ate them all. The sweet creaminess of the chocolate made her glaze over. Her senses mellowed, and her room began to look impressionistic and wavy, like the Monet Water Lily paintings they'd seen slides of in art class. Eating the donut and the Chunkys made her hands feel warm and relaxed as pleasure spread through her.

When her mother announced that dinner was ready,

Phoebe changed out of her sweatshirt into an oversized T-shirt and her soft, stretchy, red leggings, and went downstairs. She dreaded going down to dinner more than ever because her father seemed to have stepped up his campaign to renovate her. Phoebe sat at the dinner table with downcast eyes, hoping that the lack of eye contact would turn the conversation away from her body. No such luck, though.

"You're not looking good. You look puffy."

Phoebe wished her father wouldn't say things like that to her. He didn't seem to care how she was feeling, only how she was looking.

"I feel fine," she said. "There's nothing wrong with me." *Except,* she thought, *it would help if you'd leave me alone.* Moments like this with her father made her want to get even fatter.

When her mother brought dinner to the table, Phoebe had the usual anxiety about eating. She felt her father was watching her every move, her every mouthful, monitoring how much she ate, how fast she ate, and whether she chewed properly. He was extremely conscious of chewing every morsel thoroughly, ever since he had photographed a famous Japanese healer called Michio Kushi, to whom chewing was next to godliness.

Phoebe was completely miserable at dinners with her family. She enjoyed eating most when she could do it alone, away from the judging eyes of others. So, when dinner was finally over, she was enormously relieved.

After she and her mother had cleared the table, Phoebe went to work out some more, this time on the treadmill. With every step, she said, "I will be thin. I will be thin. I will be thin." *Tomorrow,* she promised herself, *I will eat only a bagel. I will tell my parents that I have an upset stomach, and I'll skip dinner. Instead of eating lunch at school, I will drink two glasses of water and then go to the library. At dinner, I'll tell them I'm eating at a friend's, and go for a walk.* "I will be thin. I will be." Saying these things to herself, Phoebe at first felt excitement and resolve.

The next day, however, her resolve turned to fear when she realized the rigorous plan she had devised. She ate her morning bagel dry, with a cup of plain tea. The strong, bitter tea had an astringent quality that pinched her tongue. She missed the soothing warmth of the milk and honey that she ordinarily would have put in her tea. However, this ascetic breakfast made her feel good in another way, and she attended her morning classes feeling strong and hopeful.

At lunchtime, she sat with Jessica, who made a display of eating by picking at a small bowl of salad. Phoebe drank the two glasses of water as she had resolved she would, but she was very hungry and felt unfocused and preoccupied by thoughts of large ham-and-cheese sandwiches.

During her afternoon classes, Phoebe felt proud of herself. But, on her way home, she felt irresistibly drawn into the variety store by the Almond Joys. She ate four of them.

Once home, she had seven slices of whole-wheat bread, thickly spread with butter and honey, and drank two glasses of milk. Then she lay down on her bed—on her bloated stomach—and cried.

* * *

It took Hannah a few minutes to stop hyperventilating when she realized the full implications of having failed her biology final for the second time. It meant she'd failed biology. She'd have to repeat the course. How could this have happened to her? The humiliation soaked into her; it overflowed and spilled out, an entire ocean of humiliation, leaving her ashamed, cold and exposed.

She arrived at Kaneesha's just as Kaneesha was putting the final touches on her manicure. The girls settled themselves into Kaneesha's large, comfortable bedroom.

Hannah didn't mention how distraught she was about her failure. She was ashamed of being so in need of help, so pathetic. She didn't need anyone's help. She just needed to forget. She would think about summer. Hannah looked so pale and tense, though, that Kaneesha had to say something about it to her.

"Anything wrong?" remarked Hannah's friend.

"Yes," blurted Hannah.

"Why don't you ask Mrs. Lundquist to find you a shrink?" asked Kaneesha, getting right to the point.

"What for?" said Hannah.

"Duh, because you're barfing," answered Kaneesha. She could also have said, "You can't study. You failed the biology final twice. You know more than it's decently possible to know about the Krebs cycle, and you answered all the questions wrong. You must have lost your mind."

"What is a therapist going to do?" said Hannah. *Could she come to the house and actually padlock the door to the refrigerator? Could she restore my I.Q.?* Hannah asked herself.

"I don't know," replied Kaneesha, "but what else can you do? You gotta do something."

Just thinking about going to a therapist turned Hannah's mouth dry. Therapists always asked you about your mother. She couldn't imagine telling anyone what her mother was really like, that sometimes she was sweet to Hannah, but at other times she would strike out at her with cruel words. Her mother would tell Hannah that she was selfish, that she was not smart enough to go to college. Then the cruel moments would pass, and a few minutes later she would be telling Hannah how intelligent and talented and beautiful she was, how lovely she looked in her new beige coat, how well she played the guitar.

Hannah never knew what to expect when she was with her mother. The bad times had been very bad. At those times, she wished her mother would die. Then the good times would replace the bad, and Hannah would be left feeling guilty and confused.

❄ ❄ ❄

Jessica got home from school to find the house in need of cleaning. The kitchen floor was sticky with apple-juice spills, and dust was on all the windowsills. Even the answering machine had a film of dust across the top.

Jessica's mother had a new boyfriend, whom Jessica hated. There was a message from him on the answering machine. She thought about him with annoyance while she cleaned the house, mopping the floor with angry vigor. He was older than her mother, much older, but he didn't act like a grown-up. He acted like a big baby, and he didn't seem to have a job. Jessica wondered where all his money came from. He drove a big black Mercedes and had an oceanfront house in the Hamptons with a swimming pool and a tennis court and a three-car garage with three cars in it. He always seemed to be flying off to Aspen or London or St. Bart. He teased Matthew and told Jessica at least once a week that she was too skinny, which was none of his business. He was quite handsome and thin, with dark good looks, but Jessica thought he was disgusting. She hated the way he looked at her legs when she wore shorts. His name was Keith, and he took up all her mother's attention. Sometimes he would disappear mysteriously for weeks at a time, and her mother would cry and complain about how irresponsible he was. If she wasn't worrying about where he was when he wasn't around, she was worrying about what to wear when he was.

One day when Jessica had been moping in her room, feeling starved but resisting food, her mother came in and said, "Cheer up. What should I wear for my date with Keith? The black or the lavender?" She held up two dresses for Jessica's approval, both with spaghetti straps and scoop necks.

Jessica started to cry suddenly. Her mother dropped the dresses on the bed and rushed over to Jessica.

"What is it, honey?" asked Adrianne, sitting down next to Jessica and holding her. "Is it PMS?"

"You always think what's wrong with me is PMS," cried Jessica. "I haven't even had my period in months."

"Oh, it will come back," Adrianne assured her. "I was irregular at your age, too. Cheer up, honey. I need your support. It's not easy being a single mom." Adrianne moved away from Jessica and stood up. She picked up the dresses, focusing on them once again.

"How can you think about clothes when I'm sitting here crying?" said Jessica impatiently, sniffing away her tears.

"Well, what should I do with you?" asked Adrianne with exasperation, dropping the dresses again and sitting back down on the bed.

"Love me. Pay attention to me. I don't know," cried Jessica.

"Don't shout. Matthew will hear you," said Adrianne.

"He should hear. I'm really the person who takes care of him. What do you care? All you care about is Keith and your acting."

"Well, I have to make a living for us," argued Adrianne. "And I love you, Jess. I'm always here for you, aren't I? Didn't we just go shopping for summer outfits? Don't I drive you everywhere you need to go?"

That is true, reasoned Jessica. *My mom is there for me, and she is fun.*

"Didn't I buy you that terrific red top you're wearing?" her mother continued. "It's hard for me, as well. I need you to be here for me, too. Since Dad died, we have to support each other, Jess. I can't have you falling apart on me. So lighten up. Pull yourself together, girl. Here. Get up. Look," she said, holding up the dresses again. "Okay now, which one?"

Jessica sniffed away the last of her tears and blinked her eyes. "The black."

Phoebe was sitting in her room, looking at the latest copy of *Elle,* and thinking about her thighs. Thoughts of the beach, ever-present at this time of year, made her so anxious that she would grind her teeth all night and wake up with her jaw so sore it ached for most of the morning.

She decided to let her father recommend a therapist. She didn't know what else to do, and she had to do something. She would tell the therapist that even when she was small her father used to introduce her to people apologetically, saying, "This is Phoebe, and, as you can see, she still has some baby fat."

But Phoebe had the strangest feeling that, if she ever were to get thinner, her father would pay even less attention to her. He was always surrounded by beautiful models. If she were thin, she would just be an ordinary teenager. Maybe it was better that she was shaped like a potato. At least he noticed her.

Just thinking about the therapy made her worry, worry that the therapist would soon be forbidding her to eat pizza and potato chips. She went downstairs to the kitchen, opened the freezer, and took out a small microwaveable pizza. While it cooked, she stared into the refrigerator to see what else there was to eat in the meantime.

She considered the cookie jar on the table. It was a replica of a giant chocolate cupcake, the handle of its lid a glistening ceramic maraschino cherry. She lifted the lid and found six cellophane-wrapped chocolate-chip cookies. Her mother bought them individually wrapped so that one cookie at a time could be opened. That way, her mother reasoned, Phoebe would eat only one instead of a whole box. They treated her like some sort of cookie monster.

When the pizza was ready, it was so hot it burned her throat and the roof of her mouth, but she ate it too quickly anyway. Her mind and heart were racing, and she was aware of how tight her jeans felt around her waist and thighs. The idea of stopping her binge brought immediate gloom, however.

Phoebe sighed and looked around the large spotless kitchen, where everything seemed to be in its place except her. It was important to her parents that everything be picture-perfect, including their daughter. She noticed how the pot holders were hung on their hooks in order of size and how the spices were alphabetized. She noticed the toaster and the jar of honey in the shape of a bear, and she wanted bread and honey.

The whole-wheat bread smelled good as she slipped it out of its plastic wrapper. While she waited for it to toast, she ate a slice plain. It was soft, sweet and chewy, and had little fragments of sunflower seeds scattered throughout. When the bread was toasted, she turned the honey jar upside down and let the honey fall onto the bread. Its golden thickness spread slowly toward the crust, soaking into each tiny crevice. The toast made her thirsty, and she drank a glass of milk.

Now she wanted more: cupcakes with fluffy frosting, applesauce with cinnamon, and blueberry pie. She wanted rich beef stew and a big plate of spaghetti with parmesan cheese sprinkled generously on top. She found cheesecake in the freezer behind the ice-cube trays. She wondered if it had been purposely hidden there. She would show them. She would eat none of it.

Instead, she went into the pantry, where boxes of breakfast

cereals were lined up in a neat row. She ate the remaining half of a box of date-almond granola. It was crunchy and nutty-tasting, especially the chunks that stuck together. She ate it right out of the box, which had a photograph of a wheat field on the front, golden sheaves of wheat blowing in the wind. Staring at that picture as she chewed, she dreamed of wind blowing through her hair and herself with a slender waistline standing in that golden field, with Daryl's arm around her.

When she had finished the cereal, her stomach hurt so much that she had to lie down. She didn't even take the time to wipe the bread crumbs off the counter or put her bowl into the dishwasher.

She made sure not to look in the mirrors that lined an entire wall of her room. That was another thing she hated. All the mirrors in her house were driving her crazy. Her father said the mirrors were good because she could keep track of herself. That was why she hated them so much. She felt stuffed with self-hate. Her jeans were strangling her. *How much longer can I keep doing this to myself?* she asked herself desperately.

G ale Holland checked her watch to see if she had time to water her plants before her next client arrived. As she walked towards the large ficus in the corner, the phone rang.

"This is Phoebe McIntyre," said the young voice on the other end. Phoebe's father had given her Gale's name.

"What seems to be the problem, Phoebe?" asked Gale as she placed the pitcher of water she'd been carrying on her desk and sat down.

"I can't stop eating," said Phoebe. "Do you think you can help?" As soon as Phoebe had spoken, she wanted to sink into the floor. She didn't know if she wanted help. What would help mean? Wouldn't help mean she'd have to give up pizza, and meat-loaf sandwiches, and bread and honey?

"Do you want help?" asked Gale, writing Phoebe's name at the top of a yellow legal pad with a bright-green marker.

"Yes," replied Phoebe, realizing that it was only half true. "Yes," she repeated in a more cautious tone, "but I'm afraid of being helped, too."

"It's wonderful that you're aware of that, Phoebe," said Gale. "So, are you ready to come in or do you want to think about it a while?"

"I've been thinking about it long enough," answered Phoebe sadly. "I seem to be able to think about it best while I'm eating." Phoebe was amazed that she could be so honest with this stranger. "Can I come tomorrow? Do you have time?"

"I sure do," said Gale. "How about 3:30?"

Phoebe was horrified. *Tomorrow?* she thought in a panic. *How can I change by tomorrow? How can I eat differently as soon as tomorrow, and why did I call?*

Phoebe went into the family room and turned on the TV. Slender models tossed their heads and their hair swirled toward the camera in an ad for jeans. This was a commercial her father had filmed. The model with the swirling hair had been to Phoebe's last birthday party. When she changed the channel, a young mother was thanking Jenny Craig for helping her lose seventy-four pounds.

Phoebe didn't want to eat freeze-dried dinners or take pills. She didn't want to drink yucky protein shakes, either, and measure all her food in little plastic cups. Ugh! Just thinking about all this was making her want to eat.

She went into the kitchen again and, as she opened the refrigerator, Tom and Nicole, her poodles, raced into the room and jumped on her, wanting her to take them out to play. Phoebe felt thwarted. She wanted to be alone with sliced pineapple and heavy syrup mixed with sweet cream, but Tom and Nicole were persistent. *Poodle therapy,* thought Phoebe, *is just what I probably could use right now instead of food.*

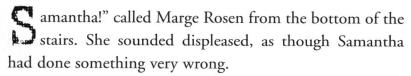

Samantha!" called Marge Rosen from the bottom of the stairs. She sounded displeased, as though Samantha had done something very wrong.

Samantha was still asleep when she heard her mother's voice that Saturday morning in June. She slowly climbed out of bed. She felt achy and weak. She knew now that she had to stand up slowly in order to prevent that funny feeling she got when she stood upright too quickly from a sitting or lying position. She had read about it in a book on anorexia. She thought it had something to do with blood pressure. She put on her pale-green robe and walked to the door of her room.

"What is it?" she slurred sleepily.

"I need to speak with you," said her mother firmly.

Samantha had never heard her mother sound so authoritative. It frightened her. Samantha had always felt she could control or manipulate her mother. The woman whose voice she had just heard sounded different.

Samantha's mother had been going to Al-Anon meetings. She knew that she needed to urge her daughter to seek help with as much leverage as she could muster, to stop trying to fix the problem herself. Two of the women at the meetings had bulimic daughters, and they'd coached Marge through the process of how she should approach Samantha.

When Samantha came downstairs, her mother said, "Let's sit in the living room. It's sunniest in there."

Samantha had always been able to project a certain intimidating attitude toward her mother to scare her off. Now, her mother had taken charge.

"Samantha," announced her mother, settling herself on the sofa, "I'm going to make an appointment for you to see a therapist. I know this is not your own choice and that it might have no effect because you aren't making the decision for yourself, but this is something I need to do for myself. So, you will go next Wednesday after school."

Samantha, horrified, said, "No way, I'm not going." It felt entirely like a dream, and Samantha didn't recognize this new mother. She hardly recognized the room they were in.

"Well," continued her mother, "you can either go see this therapist, or you're going to have to find somewhere else to live."

Samantha was flabbergasted. What had happened overnight? Was her mother throwing her out? She couldn't mean it.

"What do you mean?" asked Samantha, struggling to remain composed.

"I mean," replied Marge Rosen, smoothing her denim skirt over her knees, "that, unless you go to this appointment, you are not going to be allowed to live here anymore. You are going to be admitted to the hospital as soon as the school term is over in two weeks."

"Hospital?" asked Samantha. "What kind of hospital? I'm not sick."

"Yes, you are," said her mother firmly. "You are sick, and I am not willing to watch you get worse, so we're going to have to work at finding a way to change things."

Samantha's hands were icy. She could hardly focus her eyes. She stroked the satiny lap of her bathrobe. She looked at the furniture in her living room and didn't recognize it: the peach carpet, the stone fireplace, the Navajo blanket that was thrown over the arm of the sofa. She felt she was in the house of a stranger.

"I'm not going to any hospital," said Samantha firmly. *I can argue my way out of this,* she told herself.

"Well, if you're not going to the hospital, then you're going to have to go to the therapist. It's one or the other. Which is it?" asked her mother.

Samantha said nothing. She would try the silent treatment. She was fairly certain that, even with this new mother, the silent treatment would work very well. She listened to the sounds of the morning, the dog barking next door, the soft sounds of traffic, a distant lawn mower.

Her mother seemed entirely composed, waiting patiently. She didn't change her position or fidget anxiously.

Samantha's fear was building.

"Well, which is it?" asked her mother, looking at her watch.

This new mother unsettled Samantha. "The therapist," said Samantha, without thinking. She realized she'd been beaten in this battle, but she'd win the war. Going to the therapist didn't mean she'd have to talk or listen or eat.

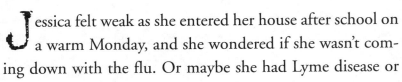

Jessica felt weak as she entered her house after school on a warm Monday, and she wondered if she wasn't coming down with the flu. Or maybe she had Lyme disease or something. She was so hugely tired.

Even her mother's boyfriend noticed something was wrong. The night before, when they had been sitting in the kitchen drinking Diet Cokes, Keith said, "Why don't you get some help, Jessica? You seem tired all the time. You need to eat better." He was always telling her how she wasn't normal, teasing her, but this didn't sound like teasing. He sounded like a real grown-up when he'd said that.

"What kind of help do you mean?" asked Jessica, her defenses rallying.

"Help. H-E-L-P. With your eating," he said. "You never eat. All I ever see you do is drink Diet Coke. You're a scarecrow. You're a pretty scarecrow, but you're still a scarecrow, and your mom's worried about you."

"Yeah, well, *your* mother should be worried about you, too," said Jessica with bitterness.

Adrianne hadn't been in the kitchen with them.

"I don't need help," insisted Jessica. "You're the one who needs help."

"Why do I need help?" asked Keith.

"Because you're such a jerk," said Jessica. She surprised even herself when she said this.

She'd been feeling so tired that she didn't have the energy to pretend anymore. She didn't even have the energy to walk to the second floor of the house to get to her room. She couldn't imagine where she would find the strength to carry her books to school. Even with all the Diet Coke and all the caffeine in it that she depended on, she was losing some of the edge she had been able to maintain.

It was a good thing the school term was ending. She would be able to sleep late and wouldn't have to go to phys ed.

Matthew would be in day camp, so she wouldn't even have to baby-sit so much. She could rest and exercise and rest some more, and maybe even lose a little more weight.

Matthew ran into her arms and started talking to her a mile a minute about his day. Jessica smiled at the baby-sitter as she let herself out. Jessica did not have the energy for a pleasant chat with her.

Matthew let go of Jessica abruptly and ran into the living room, where he continued working with Legos. He was building a hospital. "The kind Daddy used to work in," he told Jessica.

Jessica sighed and sat down in a green kitchen chair. It was a cheerful room, but it felt lonely today. A bunch of colorful plastic utensils—a ladle, a spatula, a whisk and several slotted spoons—were stuffed into a jar. They reminded Jessica of a bouquet of flowers. But all the bright colors made her feel sad. She didn't know why. The sunshine coming through the windows made her sad, too. Tears rose up in her throat, but she swallowed hard.

The phone in its usual place on the green tile counter reminded Jessica that she had promised she would call Phoebe. The phone rang suddenly, though, and Jessica was aware of how heavy the receiver felt when she picked it up.

"Phoebe," said Jessica. "Hi. What's up? You don't sound so good." She tried to make her voice sound sympathetic, but she was irritated. The receiver felt so heavy and she had a painful stiff neck.

Jessica thought of Phoebe's bingeing with fear and disgust. If she herself were to eat, she would feel she had nothing. She would feel she was nothing.

Phoebe continued to explain about her binge and described everything she had eaten.

Jessica cradled the phone between her shoulder and her ear to free her hands so that she could make Matthew his peanut-butter–and–jelly sandwich. This was their after-school routine, and it never varied. Matthew would inspect the sandwich to make sure the peanut butter came all the way to the edges of the bread. He was meticulous in so many ways. He sharpened his crayons so that they came to perfectly sharp points. When Jessica had once asked him why he didn't use felt-tipped pens instead, he said it was because you couldn't get the same shading with a felt tip.

"I feel all falling apart inside," said Phoebe, "so I made an appointment with a—"

Before she could finish, Jessica said, "Just a minute," shifting the phone to the other shoulder and pouring a glass of milk for Matthew.

"Matt, your sandwich is ready," called Jessica and then, to Phoebe, "Phoebe, I gotta go. Matt needs me."

✳ ✳ ✳

Phoebe was apprehensive as she approached the door to Gale Holland's office on a pleasant, tree-lined street. Heathbrook, Long Island, was an upscale community, and the houses and lawns were well-kept. There was a doctor's office on the first floor of the building, a white clapboard house with a big willow tree out front. As Phoebe walked up the stairs, her agitation grew.

A very large man was leaving Gale's office just as Phoebe stepped into the waiting room. He had the look that Phoebe associated with newspaper photos of men who'd won hot-dog–eating contests at state fairs, thirty-two hot dogs within twelve minutes. The strange thing, Phoebe thought, was that he was handsome. His blue eyes looked so kind, and he smiled at Phoebe as he moved past her.

Phoebe sat in an upholstered chair, a wing chair covered in dark-blue brocade. The oriental carpet in dark reds and blues looked worn and relaxed, like faded jeans. There were three other wing chairs in the room, one dark green, one deep rose, and one a deep mustard yellow. There was also a large, low, dark-wood table on which there were several magazines Phoebe had never seen: *Big Beautiful Woman*,

Vegetarian Times, The Harvard Medical Letter and *Yoga Journal.*

In *Vegetarian Times,* she noticed an article entitled "Eat More and Lose Weight." Just as she started to read it, a door opened and a tall woman with a welcoming smile leaned out and said, "Phoebe?" She put her hand out and Phoebe extended hers, as Gale smiled warmly at her.

Phoebe felt a mixture of terror and relief as she followed Gale into the large, airy room. She sat in one of the armchairs in front of the fireplace and examined the high-ceilinged room with light streaming in through French doors that opened onto a terrace fringed with hanging and standing plants. A glass vase on the uncluttered desk was filled with yellow irises.

"I'll be right back," Gale said as soon as Phoebe was seated. Gale crossed the room and went out through a door that looked like a big shutter.

Phoebe reflected on Gale's appearance. Her clothes looked casual—black jeans, black cowboy boots and a soft-looking pink T-shirt. Her hair was short, the color of butterscotch and she wore no makeup except for a hint of lip gloss. She wore small, silver, hoop earrings and a silvery Timex watch, exactly like Phoebe's. It was comforting to Phoebe to see that Gale was not skinny, but she wasn't fat either. *Jessica would probably think of Gale as fat,* thought

Phoebe, *but really Gale just looks normal.* She had a beautiful smile, with a dimple and gray eyes.

Gale came back, carrying a plastic bottle full of water and two pink paper cups. "Would you like a glass of water?" she asked as she sat down in the chair facing Phoebe's.

"Okay," said Phoebe, who wasn't thirsty, but wanted to say yes to Gale.

Gale poured out the water and handed Phoebe a cup from which Phoebe dutifully sipped.

"Now," said Gale, settling down in her chair, "what seems to be the problem, Phoebe?"

Phoebe did not know where to begin. She was glad she had taken the cup of water because now she sipped it, gathering her thoughts. There were so many things to tell about, and they'd been going on for so many years, for what felt like Phoebe's whole life. How could she sum it up in a sentence or a paragraph, or even in ten years of continuous talking? Suddenly, she was overwhelmed by it. Her eyes filled with tears, and she fought to keep them from brimming over.

"It must feel very intense to be here, huh?" asked Gale.

That's an understatement, thought Phoebe.

"I don't know where to begin," she said, putting the cup of water down on the small table beside her chair.

"Well," said Gale, uncrossing her long legs, "why don't you tell me why you called me yesterday and not last month or next week, but yesterday particularly?"

"Well," said Phoebe, gathering her composure as she struggled to focus her thoughts, "I had this big eating binge." She stopped. She didn't know if she wanted to tell about this.

"Bigger than usual?" said Gale, obviously unsurprised by this news.

"No, about the same as usual," observed Phoebe.

"So, how come you called then?"

"I'm so fed up, I guess," sighed Phoebe. "I'm just so tired of feeling horrible about myself, and I'm tired of my father always criticizing, and I'm tired of having all my friends tell me how awfully afraid they are of being fat like me, whom they obviously consider disgusting."

"How does it feel to think that your friends are disgusted by you, Phoebe?" asked Gale.

Phoebe's eyes filled again. Gale waited. Phoebe swallowed hard, but the tears still flowed.

Finally, Gale said, "How does it feel to be you, Phoebe?"

Now Phoebe began to sob. Feelings she didn't realize she had and didn't know were so intense spilled out as tears streamed down her cheeks. Her sorrow was so deep it didn't seem it could ever be washed away, even if she cried for ten years; her sorrow was so big that no amount of attention and skill could ever erase it.

Gale waited for a minute or two and then leaned forward, offering Phoebe a pink box of Kleenex from which Phoebe pulled three tissues.

"You have some pretty strong feelings inside," remarked Gale thoughtfully. "Three-tissue feelings. Do you want to tell me about them?"

Phoebe nodded, blotting her cheeks with the tissues. "I know I have a lot of friends and everything," said Phoebe, sniffling. "I do well in school. It doesn't seem hard for me to do so well. It's not an effort. I'm healthy. I can have any clothes I want . . . but I'm so miserable when I open my eyes in the morning and I realize I'm still me. I just don't want to be me anymore. I'm so completely sick of myself." She hesitated. "It's almost as though I didn't know I knew these things," she continued. "They were like secrets I was not allowed to tell myself."

"There's a lot of denial about such uncomfortable thoughts and feelings," observed Gale. "We need some denial to get through the day, a certain amount of it anyway."

"Yes, that's it," agreed Phoebe. "I needed to keep those things secret. Also, my parents are so awful to me. I mean, they don't think they're cruel or anything. They probably think they're just nice, normal parents because they give me everything, like a CD player and my own VCR, and stuff like that. But I would rather they'd tell me I looked nice or that I'm terrific in some way. They never tell me anything like that." She hesitated and looked at her feet in their white Nikes. "I never get hugged, either," she added. "Oprah said it was really important to get hugged." Her eyes were filling up with tears again.

Gale sat quietly for a moment. Then she said, "How does it feel to have parents who haven't told you nice things about yourself?"

Phoebe began to sob again. "It feels as though they don't love me, as though I'm not worth anything," cried Phoebe. "I feel so empty, so worthless. I know there's something really wrong with me, something that can never, ever be fixed, not even if I lose weight. I'm so tired, just so tired of all the longing."

"You've been suffering for a long time, Phoebe, haven't you?" said Gale softly.

"I want so badly to feel like other people, like I belong," wailed Phoebe, taking another tissue out of the pink box that Gale had placed on the table beside her.

"Do you know that one of my friends actually said to me, 'I'd rather die than get fat'? She would actually rather die than be like me! How is that supposed to make me feel? Don't people think I have feelings, too?"

"How does that make you feel?" asked Gale.

"Disgusting! Miserable! Like a big, brown, shapeless

potato!" Phoebe began to cry again. "Have you ever been fat?" asked Phoebe, sobbing.

"Why is that important to you?" asked Gale.

"Because I can't imagine how you could possibly know what it feels like to be me," answered Phoebe, crumpling up the tissues in her lap.

"You know, Phoebe, everyone has feelings of differentness at one time or another, and these are always painful things, especially at your age," said Gale. "We can talk about me sometime, but right now we need to concentrate on you."

"So, what do we do now?" asked Phoebe.

"What do you want to do?" answered Gale.

"Well," said Phoebe with some anxiety, "I don't want to not eat what I'm used to eating."

"Good," agreed Gale. "I don't want you to change a thing about what you're eating. I just want you to write about it. Do you think you could do that this week?"

"What do you mean by 'write about it'?" asked Phoebe suspiciously.

"Well, I've found that it's helpful for people to write down what they are eating each day, sort of a food diary. How do you feel about that?"

Phoebe looked doubtful. "I don't know. That would make me pretty uncomfortable. It's one of the secrets about myself I'm not supposed to know, if you know what I mean. But I guess I could do it, if you think it would help." Phoebe didn't want to say no to Gale, but she also felt afraid of yes. "Do I have to count calories or fat or anything?" asked Phoebe.

"No," replied Gale. "Just write down what you're eating. How about that?"

"But how can I ever get thinner if I don't change anything about the food?" asked Phoebe, her anxiety mounting.

"We have to go really slow," answered Gale.

As Phoebe walked to the bus, her mind was tangled with a confusion of excited thoughts and feelings. She was happy and tired and sad and hungry. Her head was spinning, and she wanted most of all to calm down. But the only way she'd ever known how to calm herself down was by eating something, lots of something.

She decided to pick up the bus at a later stop and walked to the pizza place on the next street, where she ordered two slices of pizza with sausage and extra cheese. She felt guilty at first, but she recalled what Gale had said, "Do the same thing that you have been doing with food this week," and she felt suddenly lighthearted. She enjoyed eating the pizza more than she had enjoyed eating anything in recent memory.

* * *

Samantha cleaned and vacuumed her room for the second time that afternoon. It was the day she had agreed to go and see Gale Holland. She had set her alarm for 4:30 A.M. so she could exercise before going to school, spending an hour and a half on the treadmill. Then, at 6:00, she'd felt so panicky that she dusted her already dust-free room, straightened out the two dozen pairs of shoes at the bottom of her closet and polished her nails blue.

When she was through, she dressed in her black, satiny bell-bottoms, her zebra-striped platform shoes and a white tank top (she wore a green satin shirt over this to hide the marks she'd made on her shoulder), and went downstairs to the kitchen.

There, she took a bowl out of the cabinet and opened a box of cornflakes. She sprinkled three of the cornflakes into the bowl, opened a container of milk and spilled a few drops into the bowl. Then she set the bowl in the sink with a spoon and filled it partially with water. The effect pleased her. She gloated at how easy it was to fool her parents into thinking she'd eaten.

Later that day, after school, she walked to the bus, trying not to think of the appointment she had with Gale Holland. She had told no one about having to go, but she wondered what Gale would say to her, how she would try to trick her into changing. Of course she wouldn't give in, no matter what.

There was no way anyone would make her eat if she didn't want to, though she was hungry.

Gale sounded like a fat name to Samantha. That was one thing Samantha liked about herself, her name. *Samantha* sounded thin to her, like a sleek, black cat, lean with no extra flesh. *Gale Holland,* on the other hand, sounded plump.

Samantha hesitated before she rang the bell. At first, she thought she might be at the wrong place because the building looked cheery and welcoming, with its weeping willow tree and yellow irises blooming in the front yard, but then she saw the name *Gale Holland* on a brass plaque beside the front door. The street was filled with the beautiful fragrance of freshly cut grass, but Samantha didn't notice this. She was completely preoccupied with fears about what would happen inside.

Her mother had become really tough. Samantha didn't understand why she didn't pay more attention to her sister, Patty, who at ten was almost as fat as Alexa. Samantha had offered to help Patty with a diet, but she just wasn't interested.

Gale buzzed Samantha in, and Samantha found herself in Gale's comfortable waiting room, where she paged through magazines without seeing anything. Her hands were like icicles, and her mouth had that familiar, unpleasant, sour taste.

When Gale came out of her office to greet her, Samantha was surprised to see her looking so casual and trim. She wore a filmy, black skirt with sandals and a white T-shirt.

"Please sit wherever you like," said Gale when Samantha had followed her into her office.

Gale noticed that as Samantha walked to a chair in front of the fireplace her black, satiny bell-bottoms sagged in back and the green shirt Samantha wore hung about her sloping shoulders. She noticed the bones in Samantha's chest above the top edge of the white tank top and that Samantha held onto the arm of the chair as she lowered herself into it.

"You look as though something hurts, Samantha," observed Gale.

"I'm fine," insisted Samantha.

"Would you like a glass of water?"

"No," said Samantha firmly.

"Well, why don't you tell me why you're here today, Samantha?"

"I came because my mother said if I didn't she would put me into a hospital," Samantha explained in an irritated tone.

"What is your mother concerned about?" asked Gale.

"I have no idea," replied Samantha, lying.

"Well, I'll bet it has to do with your eating," said Gale.

"I don't want to talk about it."

"Well, that's fine," said Gale. "We can just sit together then."

This may not be as easy as I thought it would be, mused Samantha. *She doesn't seem intimidated by silence, but she's not going to make me talk and, if she does, there's no way she can make me eat. I said I'd come; I didn't say I'd eat.*

Samantha sat. Gale drank her water and then poured herself another cup from the plastic bottle on the small table beside her chair. She drank the water slowly, not seeming to be disturbed by Samantha's refusal to talk.

Gale placed her empty cup on the table after holding it for a while and said finally, "Well, I'm ready to talk now, Samantha."

"Well, I don't want to talk," said Samantha.

"I didn't say you had to talk," said Gale. "I said I was ready to talk. So I'm going to tell you a little bit about yourself. You're a junior or a senior in high school, and you're probably a very good student. You spend most of your time thinking about what you can do to lose more weight. You lie to your parents all the time about what you're eating. You may have had a boyfriend, but at some point I'll bet he left you because he was tired of how involved you were in food and in your body. It's possible that you have engaged in acts of self-mutilation, cutting yourself possibly, and you are extremely neat and tidy, cleaning your room much too often, maybe even cleaning the rest of the house, as well."

"How do you know all this?" asked Samantha, surprising even herself with this remark. She was surprised that Gale could know so much about her. How could this have happened? Maybe her mother had talked to Gale. "Did my mother speak to you?"

"No," replied Gale, "your mother got my number from Mrs. Antonio, but she didn't tell me anything about you when she made the appointment for you. I asked her not to tell me anything except to describe her own feelings about the situation."

"My mother didn't tell you anything about me, then?" probed Samantha, feeling confused and anxious.

"No," repeated Gale.

"Then how did you know so much about me?" asked Samantha, annoyed at herself for talking so much, for talking at all.

"Because I have been doing this work for long enough to know many girls with your eating and lifestyle patterns. You have a lot in common. By the way, I need for you to have a complete physical exam. I can't work with you unless I know you are being looked after medically."

Samantha shifted in her chair. It hurt when she sat for any length of time, even in this upholstered chair. She was annoyed about this physical-exam thing, but what choice did she have? If she refused to go, Gale wouldn't work with her, and if Gale wouldn't work with her, she'd have to go to a hospital.

Samantha wanted to talk some more, to ask Gale more questions, but she was displeased with herself for talking so much already, so she used her will to resist speaking, the way she used her will to resist eating when she was hungry. She sat and absorbed all the things Gale had told her about herself and the information coming from outside herself felt like food to her. It made her anxious, and she felt stuffed, as though she had eaten too much.

"It makes you feel very special and powerful not to eat, doesn't it?" continued Gale, after they had sat in silence for a few more minutes. "Somewhere deep inside you want to be normal, but you also hate the idea of being ordinary or average, so you think you will probably always be sick when it comes to feeding yourself. You will always feel set apart, and there will be good feelings associated with this, feelings of being special. But there will be bad feelings, too, feelings of being terribly lonely and different. You will be frightened that you have drifted so far away from normal that no one could ever hear you, even if you cried."

Samantha began to feel weepy. She struggled successfully, though, to hold back tears.

"How do you know all these things?" asked Samantha, surprised to hear herself talking again.

"Because," said Gale, "I have thought about these things for a long time, much longer than you have." She reached for her appointment book, which sat on the table beside her chair. They sat quietly for a few more minutes.

Gale opened her appointment book, consulted it briefly, and said, "How about coming to see me next week again at this same time?"

That's all you'll do is see me, thought Samantha, *because you won't hear me.*

When Samantha had gone and Gale was getting ready to meet with her group, she thought about how painfully thin Samantha was and how it might be a good idea for her to have group treatment.

The phone rang just before 6:00. The young voice sounded frightened. It was Hannah.

Propped against four pillows on her bed, her journal balanced on her knees, Phoebe wrote:

```
Don't know why,
      don't know why,
            don't know why
                  I ate the pie.
```

The poodles, Tom and Nicole, jumped onto the bed, snuggling close to her, one on each side. She had gotten the dogs soon after she'd met Tom Cruise when her father had photographed him. Phoebe wrote a brief film script about Tom Cruise and herself in her journal. It went like this:

TOM: Phoebe, it's taken me weeks to find you. I thought I'd never see you again.

PHOEBE: Tom, we can't. What about Nicole?

TOM: Oh, she's too tall for me, Phoeb. She's positively giraffic. It's you I long for. I sit at home looking at Nicole's long legs, sinewy arms and slender waist, tormented to be without your reassuring bulk. I can kiss the top of your head. I can only reach to her collarbone.

He moves toward Phoebe with his eyes glistening, enfolding her, holding her close. He can't quite get his arms completely around her, though, because she has her backpack on.

PHOEBE: But Tom, your career!

TOM: Oh, yeah, that, but let me hold you just once without your backpack. Then I'll go.

* * *

School was finally over, and the Maple Ridge High students were freed from the prisons created by their schedules.

The first Saturday after the end of the term, Lacey called Samantha to see if she wanted to go bathing-suit shopping with her. Shopping for bathing suits was horrible, not something you wanted to do by yourself.

When Samantha answered the phone, Lacey could hear the vacuum cleaner in the background. "Turn off that machine, Sam, I can't hear you!"

"Oh, all right," said Samantha.

"You clean your room too much," said Lacey. "Enough is enough! How do you have time to exercise when you're vacuuming all the time?"

"I get up early, and I wear my ankle weights while I'm vacuuming," replied Samantha in a rare moment of candor.

"Oh, what a good idea," agreed Lacey.

Samantha felt apprehensive about talking to Lacey or to any of her friends because she didn't want to tell them about her visit to see Gale Holland, but it was all she could think about. She couldn't imagine not talking about it.

She turned off the vacuum cleaner and sat wearily on her bed. Everything in her room looked stiff and unwelcoming. Even the stuffed zebras were arranged in such a deliberate way that they did not invite cuddling.

"So, what are you doing today?" asked Lacey.

"Oh, I don't know," said Sam. "I just woke up. It's our first Saturday without homework. There are a million things I could do."

"So, you just woke up, and the first thing you're doing is vacuuming? That's on your list of a million things? It should be on the bottom."

"What's wrong with vacuuming?" replied Samantha defensively.

Lacey sighed dramatically. "Oh, Sam, you can be so boring sometimes."

"Thanks a lot."

"I called to see if you wanted to go into town to do some bathing-suit shopping," said Lacey, inspecting her nails for chips and ragged cuticles. She frowned at them critically.

I don't ever want to see myself in a bathing suit for as long as I live, thought Samantha. *My body looks so scrawny, but it feels so fat. I feel even worse after seeing Gale. I just know she's going to try to make me eat, I know she is. I have to get skinnier so that if I do gain weight I still won't be fat.*

"So, will you come with me?" asked Lacey impatiently.

"All right," said Samantha.

When she hung up, she continued thinking about what Gale had said, how she had known all about her, all about the cleaning and the cutting. She felt, because Gale had recited all those well-guarded secrets so casually, that she was no longer special and that she could never have any privacy anymore.

She heard her mother moving around downstairs and remembered her mother's new take-charge attitude. Samantha shuddered to think of what other changes her mother might be cooking up. She turned on the vacuum cleaner and drowned out these thoughts with its noise. She smoothed the vacuum over the carpeting, way into the corners to capture all the dust, every speck.

Hannah?" said Gale, as she came out of her office. "Hi, I'm Gale."

Hannah shook Gale's extended hand and followed her into her office. It was a bright day, and Hannah was wearing shorts that showed her long, slender legs and an oversized T-shirt that hid the bones in her chest.

"What seems to be the problem, Hannah?" asked

Gale, after they had settled themselves into their chairs.

"I failed my biology exam twice," admitted Hannah. "I have never failed anything in my life. I have one of the highest grade-point averages in our school, usually."

"What's going on in your life, Hannah? Anything special?"

"Nothing special," said Hannah, "except these failures."

"Has anything unusual happened to you lately, anything having to do with loss or change?"

"Oh, that kind of special," said Hannah. "Well, my mother died just under two years ago. That's why the guidance counselor thought of sending me to see you."

"Ah," said Gale. She remained silent for a moment and then, since Hannah said nothing more, let another moment go by.

"Is that the sort of special you meant?" inquired Hannah.

"Exactly," said Gale. She let another quiet moment pass.

Hannah noticed the big painting of green grapes above the fireplace. She could taste their juicy sweetness, could feel their coolness. Her neck muscles tensed.

"Were you close to your mother?" asked Gale finally.

"I guess so. I don't know how close other girls are to their mothers. She was anorexic." Hannah hadn't meant to talk about this. Fear and confusion came suddenly. Hannah swallowed hard and crossed her legs.

Gale didn't say anything.

Hannah's mind raced around, searching frantically for something to say to ease her discomfort. Finding it unbearable to be in the silence, she plunged in. "I was ashamed of my mother's problem. She was so emaciated at the end. She had cancer, so it was kind of natural, but I knew . . . I knew. I was more ashamed that I didn't do anything to help her." Hannah looked down at the pattern of faded flowers that covered the carpet beneath her feet.

"What do you think you could have done?" asked Gale softly.

"I don't know," said Hannah. "I was afraid to make her more uncomfortable. I was afraid to make it worse."

"I can understand that," agreed Gale.

Hannah looked at the certificates and diplomas on Gale's wall and wondered if these documents would help her. She looked at the lilacs in the pink glass vase on the desk, at the sunlight slanting across the wall. A feeling of safety overcame her. It was not a familiar feeling, yet she recognized what it was. She started to cry with relief.

"You know," she said, "I felt I could have saved her. I'm horrible because I didn't try."

"There was nothing you could have done to save your mother," said Gale. "We have no control over other people. We hardly have control over ourselves most of the time."

"I know," said Hannah, blowing her nose, "but I keep

thinking about it anyway. It just goes around and around in my mind, over and over, and the only way I can stop it is by eating everything in sight, and then I worry about that."

* * *

Phoebe turned the pages of *Teen People* magazine and thought about what she had eaten that day: some cereal with a banana in the morning, followed by a big glob of peanut butter eaten off a spoon. She didn't know how to measure the glob, so she estimated it to be about two table-spoons' worth. When she looked up peanut butter in the paperback nutrition counter she had gotten at the new Barnes & Noble in town, she was horrified. One tablespoon of peanut butter had one hundred calories and seven grams of fat. Even though Gale had said not to bother counting any-thing, Phoebe was dismayed that she hadn't looked up peanut butter before she had eaten that big glob of it. She'd thought peanut butter was a health food. Now she was afraid of it.

She felt some anxiety about what she'd eaten for lunch that day as well: a tuna-salad sandwich with a mysterious amount of mayonnaise and a baked apple with some sweet cream drizzled on it. She was becoming more afraid of food than ever.

After dinner, which had been a piece of broiled fish with mashed potatoes and green beans, along with two fat-free cookies, Phoebe had sneaked downstairs and had five more of the cookies with a glass of milk. It was an act of enormous self-control that she hadn't eaten the whole box.

Phoebe had decided to tell her parents about Gale when her father got back from his location shoot the next day. He would, she knew, be full of images of skinny models, and Phoebe felt that after he'd spent time with these impossibly beautiful women she would appear to him to be even more squat and chubby.

The thing was she didn't want her father to love her just because she was going to be thin; she wanted him to love her for her Phoebe-ness, whatever that might mean: for her friendliness, her sense of humor, her talent for whistling, and not because she looked a certain way or wore a certain size.

On Monday, she was going to start work at her father's photography studio and help keep the busy studio running smoothly while the regular staff had their summer vacations. Phoebe was nervous about working there because she knew how her father always apologized for her when he introduced her to people.

She looked in her closet for just the right thing to wear for her first day and finally settled on an old T-shirt she loved with Pink Floyd on the front. It was black and the rainbow colors in the band's name were great. She examined herself in the mirror and, for the sixteenth time, wondered if she should cut her hair.

Daryl had asked her if he could come to the studio some-time during the summer to see how it worked. Just thinking about Daryl terrified Phoebe and made her think of Devil Dogs.

Gale had said that if Phoebe wanted to call with a question or a request for support, she should not hesitate. Phoebe dialed Gale's number, but the line was busy.

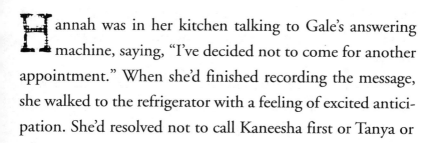

Hannah was in her kitchen talking to Gale's answering machine, saying, "I've decided not to come for another appointment." When she'd finished recording the message, she walked to the refrigerator with a feeling of excited antici-pation. She'd resolved not to call Kaneesha first or Tanya or

Doug when she knew she was going to binge. They'd made her promise, but she wasn't going to do it.

She took out some butter, some English muffins and a jar of grape jelly, and popped two halves of a muffin into the toaster. While waiting for them to toast, she ate a container of vanilla yogurt. When the muffin was ready, she placed another one in the toaster and buttered the first one, being generous with the butter, watching as it melted into the warm muffin, dripping from the peaks of its surface into the valleys. She spooned grape jelly, shimmering and jewel-like, onto the first slice and took a big bite. The intense sweetness made her teeth twinge at first, but, by the time she was into the second half, she began to have that comforting flat feeling that was the reason she ate this way. Hannah ate two more of the muffins, not as slowly as she ate the first one, and then looked into the refrigerator for her second course.

As she was about to start on some potato chips, the phone rang. She let the answering machine pick up and heard Kaneesha's voice, "Han, where are you? Are you there? Are you eating? Are you listening to that incredible Americana album?"

Hannah felt sick with herself for avoiding a friend who was so kind to her, but she would have to throw up now if she didn't want to look like a blimp.

She went to the bathroom on the second floor, locked the door, and got on her knees in front of the toilet. *This is like a weird form of worship,* she thought. The hard white tile hurt her knees. The blue water in the toilet smelled fresh and clean. She always made sure the toilets were clean since she was continually putting her face in them. That's where she belonged, she thought, in the toilet. That's where she and her life belonged.

She put her fingers down her throated, gagged and coughed violently, but nothing else happened. She was unable to bring up the food. Her eyes teared, her throat burned and ached, and her knuckles were sore from where her teeth had cut into them. She drank three glasses of water as quickly as she could and tried again, but again she couldn't get her stomach to give back the food. She was more afraid than she could ever remember, except for the day she had come home from school and her father told her that her mother was dead.

*   *   *

Samantha arrived at Gale's office almost fifteen minutes late. After parking her Mazda, she had done some window shopping to delay her arrival. This way, she reasoned, she wouldn't have to sit there in that deadly silence for quite as long.

She had dressed carefully. She concealed her body in layers of tank tops covered by a big plaid shirt, one much too large for her petite figure and too warm for the summer day.

Gale came into the waiting room and greeted her with a smile. "How are you feeling, Samantha?" asked Gale.

Samantha was aching all over. Her back and neck hurt so much she could barely hold up her head, but she affected a tone of boredom, as though her fatigue was not something to make a big deal about. "I'm tired, so I don't feel much like talking," she said.

"Okay," said Gale, "don't talk then."

This time, Gale didn't talk either.

Samantha looked at the large painting of green grapes over the fireplace. They looked delicious, juicy and plump. There were little droplets of water on them that looked cold and refreshing. Now Samantha was intensely thirsty, but she wouldn't ask for a glass of water. She was hungry and was getting that headache.

She longed to go home, to call Lacey and Alexa, to look

at her zebras. She longed to vacuum her room, craved the soothing whir of the machine that made her forget her hunger and the fears that she couldn't name but that followed her everywhere.

She willed herself to say nothing. She studied her blue chair. Its brocade upholstery had swirls of flowers and stems woven into the fabric and she concentrated on the line of one of the stems to distract herself from thoughts of food. If she let herself think about food, it was only a few steps before the thought might turn into an action.

She had an idea. She took a copy of *Vogue* out of her backpack. "Look," she said, holding up the magazine and pointing to the model on the cover. The smallness of the model's waist looked impossible, as though no human being's internal organs could fit into a space that narrow. All the equipment of digestion and reproduction couldn't possibly arrange itself into such a small area. The model's long, bony legs looked ill-equipped to keep her upright. The joints of her elbows protruded further than the outlines of her forearms. "I'm no skinnier than she is," said Samantha.

"She looks pretty skinny," observed Gale.

"What I meant to say," said Samantha, "was that she looks skinnier than me, and you don't see her in any hospital. She's on the beach on some island. I look like a blimp when I put on a bathing suit, if you want to know the truth."

The hunger had turned from a widening emptiness in the center of her body to a dull ache that made it uncomfortable for her to sit up.

"You know you're not fat, don't you?" said Gale.

"But, if I'm not fat, then why do I feel that I am?"

"It's because you don't feel fully formed as a person, Samantha. It's as though you're not Jell-O yet. That's a fat *feeling,* not a fact."

Samantha was momentarily surprised, though she didn't want to show it. Something in what Gale had said had struck a place of truth inside. It startled her, and she took a quick, involuntary breath. Along with the breath, she took in the remark that Gale had just made. She took it in and tucked it away to think about later in private.

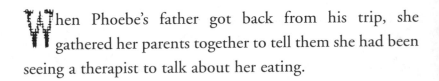

When Phoebe's father got back from his trip, she gathered her parents together to tell them she had been seeing a therapist to talk about her eating.

Her father was elated. He hugged her and said, "'Atta girl! I knew I could count on you!"

It was the most positive thing Phoebe had ever heard her father say to her, and she was overjoyed. She spent most of the rest of the weekend singing "Ain't No Mountain High Enough."

When she began working at her father's photography studio, she found she had been wrong about her father not wanting to introduce her to anyone as his daughter. He seemed proud of her now and, whenever a new client from an ad agency or a new model came in, he would put his arm around Phoebe's shoulders and say, "This is my daughter," with pride. Phoebe felt more a part of her own family when she was at the studio with her father now, as though she finally belonged somewhere.

During one of Phoebe's therapy appointments later that week, Gale said, "Well, Phoebe, I think it's time to talk about reducing the amount of fat you're eating. What do you think?"

"Ooh, I don't know," said Phoebe doubtfully. "I would have to look at the fat-gram counter every time I wanted to eat anything."

"Yep, you probably would at first, or you would have to read the label of the thing you wanted to eat. It's like having a budget. Later on, we can talk about healthier choices and exercise and how sugar behaves in your body, but for now let's go slow. What do you think?"

"I guess I could try it," said Phoebe apprehensively.

"That's all we need," said Gale encouragingly. "For this to work, all we need is for you to be willing to try things. I have another idea about something you might be willing to try. It's group therapy. What do you think?"

"Do you think it might help me?" asked Phoebe suspiciously.

"Yes," said Gale, "it helps if you're willing to be helped, and I think you are, Phoebe. Want to give it a try?"

"When is group?" inquired Phoebe.

"My group meets right here at 6:00 tonight. You could start tonight or you could wait and start next week."

"Would I still be seeing you alone?" asked Phoebe.

"Of course. We'll still be having private sessions, too."

Phoebe deliberated. She could wait until next week and be nervous the whole time, or she could just jump right in before she had too long to torture herself with dread.

"I'll start tonight," she decided. "If I hate it, do I have to keep going?"

"No, of course not," replied Gale, "but, if you do hate it, you will have to come back to group just once more to tell the group how you feel."

When Phoebe came out of Gale's office to wait for group to start, Faye was already in the waiting room. She looked up at Phoebe as she sat down in the chair closest to the door. Faye was very skinny, a tall, pale woman who looked to be in her thirties. She had on the uniform of a nurse or something having to do with doctors: white pants, a white V-neck top and white gum-soled shoes. She was so thin that Phoebe could see the blue of her veins below her collarbone and blue lines running down the insides of her arms. Faye had sad eyes and graying brown hair. She reminded Phoebe of an injured bird.

Soon, a short, stocky boy arrived to join them.

Faye said, "Hi, Billy." Here she coughed violently. "How goes it?" Her voice broke and cracked alarmingly.

"It goes well, it goes well," said Billy cheerfully, sitting beside Phoebe. He turned to her immediately and extended his hand. "Hi. I'm Bill," he announced. "Who are you?"

Before Phoebe could answer, in came a trim, athletic-looking fellow. He had a nice smile. When he sat down, Faye said, "Scott, you look great. You're finally gaining some weight."

Billy turned back to Phoebe. "As I was saying . . . where were we?" He smiled.

"I'm Phoebe."

Scott was looking at her, so she said again, this time to him, "Hi. I'm Phoebe. I'm new."

"I know," remarked Scott. "I could tell."

Phoebe felt silly. *What a ridiculous thing to say,* she thought. *I'm new.*

Gale came into the waiting room then and said, "We have a new member tonight: Phoebe. Next week, we probably will have two more new members."

"Let's go around the room and introduce ourselves to Phoebe," suggested Gale when the group members had settled into chairs around the fireplace. "Tell her why you're here, whether group has helped you, all that stuff, or, if you hate group, explain to her why she should never come back here ever again."

They all laughed.

Billy spoke first. He said he had come because he had always been fat, that he couldn't stop eating.

Scott said, "I come here because for years I was throwing up in order to make a certain weight for wrestling. Now that I'm thirty, I'm still doing it, even though I'm not wrestling anymore. I've been coming for about a year, and I'm just beginning to keep some of my food. I'm afraid of getting fat."

Frightfully thin Faye was next. She spoke so softly and with such a gravelly voice that Phoebe could hardly hear her. She seemed to have difficulty breathing, gasping for breath every few words. Her neck looked as fragile as a baby bird's. "I've stopped . . . throwing up, and I've gained . . .

weight," said Faye with difficulty. She said she was having trouble eating anything, afraid she would get fat.

"Now it's your turn, Phoebe," said Gale, taking Phoebe by surprise.

Phoebe looked so startled that the group laughed, and then Phoebe laughed, too. "I didn't expect to have to say anything so soon," she admitted.

"Well," said Gale, "do you want to tell the group how you happened to come to see me?"

Phoebe told the group about her father, about her eating, about her friends who were all thin, and about her job at the photo studio where she would envy the skinny models all day long.

"I know how that feels," said Faye raspily. "I feel like that all the time when I look at magazines."

"But you are skinny," said Phoebe with amazement.

"Oh, I'm not skinny," argued Faye. "I'm huge."

"Imagine how I feel," added Billy.

"How do you feel?" said Gale to them both.

Billy said, "I feel like a worthless pile of mud."

"I feel like a big ball of Crisco," added Phoebe sadly.

It was so good to hear other people feeling the same way she did that she wanted to jump up and hug everyone.

Faye said, gasping after each few words, "I saw my father on Father's Day." She coughed and related her story slowly.

"It was so hard. I wanted to strangle him, but I also wanted him to hug me." She hesitated. Phoebe could see that she was replaying the scene in her mind, seeing it.

Faye sighed. "Of course neither thing happened," she gasped. She hesitated again.

The feeling in the group shifted. Phoebe could sense it. These people had heard about Faye's father before. They were feeling along with her.

Faye's eyes took on a dreamy, glazed-over look, and she squeezed them shut. Tears seeped out around the edges. She wiped them away with the backs of her hands like a child might have.

"I swear I feel as though I'm seven years old around him," she continued, sniffling, gasping. "I just want so badly to please him, and all he winds up doing is hurting me again."

"What happened this time?" asked Scott.

"He said I looked like a slut in what I was wearing," explained Faye.

"Why don't you choose someone to be your father, Faye? It sounds like you might want to get angry now," suggested Gale.

"Billy, you be Dad," said Faye. "I feel like I want to hit you already."

"Oh," said Gale, "if you want to hit something, let's change our strategy here. Maybe you'd like to hit a few pillows and do some screaming at your dad. Do you?"

"I feel funny with that pillow-punching stuff," said Faye.

"I know," said Gale, "everyone feels funny about it, but it's really helpful once you get into it and past the embarrassment part."

"C'mon, Faye," said Scott encouragingly. "I did it last time, and it felt amazing. Once you start smacking 'em, you really get into it."

"Oh, all right," agreed Faye reluctantly, breathily.

She stood and followed Gale to the far end of the room where Gale piled some big pink pillows on the floor and braced them against the wall. Then she took a red foam-rubber bat out of the chest beneath the window. Gale reminded Faye of the correct way to hold it so that Faye wouldn't hurt her hands or wrists when she hit the pillows with it.

"Okay," said Gale, "now take a deep breath and start hitting those pillows rhythmically. Bring the bat down from way over your head and let it land firmly in the center of the pillows. Okay? Go!"

Faye began to smack the pillows with the red bat. She started slowly, and the sound was of a long, mellow, rhythmic drumbeat.

Phoebe watched this procedure with fascination and

alarm. Would she have to do this in order to learn to eat better? She hoped not.

After a minute or two, the drumbeats accelerated. Faye began to put energy into the strokes of the bat. Phoebe didn't know if Faye had that much energy.

"Okay, good, Faye. Now, give it a voice," instructed Gale. "What do you want to say to your father? Tell him. Let the pillows take your message."

Phoebe was surprised to hear what Faye had to say.

Faye brought the bat down hard onto the pillows. "I love you, you bastard!" she cried.

The bat came down harder and faster now. "I love you, and you hurt me so much! How could you hurt me like that? I hate you for hurting me so much! I just wanted you to love me back! How could you do that to me? How could you do that to someone who loved you so much, to a child, how could you? How could you? How could you?"

With every utterance of the words "how could you," Faye brought the bat down harder on the pillows, harder and harder, faster and faster, until it looked to Phoebe that Faye had lost control.

Phoebe envied Faye then. The only time Phoebe let herself lose control was when she was eating.

Hannah had decided to take a summer course in biology to make up for her twice-failed exam, and she felt out of step with her friends' schedules. She sat on her bed, turning the pages of her biology text, looking for the diagram of the heart. She was in summer school with students who hadn't done well, and she was afraid that getting low grades might be contagious. It certainly made her feel like an outcast. She was ashamed to be in summer school.

She felt even more ashamed about her interest in women. There was a girl, Kerry, in Hannah's class who had been very friendly, always coming over and starting conversations. She was tall like Hannah, but with frizzy, short, red hair and freckles. Her hazel eyes were large and fringed with pale lashes, giving her a perpetually surprised look. A year younger than Hannah, she was taking the course not because she'd failed but because she wanted to graduate early.

When Kerry looked into Hannah's eyes, Hannah felt that Kerry could see into a part of her that no one had ever seen before, not even Hannah herself. It was a wonderful part of her. It made Hannah feel trembly, and she forced herself to focus on something else.

She and Kaneesha were getting together later, and she was looking forward to this. She wrote in her journal while waiting for Kaneesha to pick her up so they could go to the movies in town.

> I feel so alone and apart, like a piece of the mainland that has broken off and drifted out to sea. I need desperately to come back, but I don't know how. I don't think this will ever go away, and I can't imagine living like this anymore.

When Kaneesha came by and walked up to Hannah's bedroom, she was surprised to see Hannah looking so gloomy. Even her clothes—black cutoffs and a red T-shirt—seemed faded and dull. Her lovely, small face with its smooth skin and her thick, wavy, brown hair were the same, but the liveliness had gone out of her big eyes.

"Hey, Han, how are you?"

"So, you're a busy working girl now," remarked Hannah, eager to get the conversation shifted away from herself.

"Yeah," answered Kaneesha, sitting on the edge of the bed. "I'm working in the glamorous world of retailing, where everyone but me is white, and nobody has crooked teeth or unwanted, problem hair."

"I know what you mean," said Hannah, getting off the bed and closing her books. Now that Kaneesha was there, Hannah felt like being alone even though she was so lonely.

"Well, you're tall and beautiful and thin," observed Kaneesha, looking envyingly at Hannah's long legs.

"I don't feel thin," admitted Hannah, scowling at herself in the mirror on her closet door. "I feel lumpy and lazy and dumb. That's what summer school does to you."

"What about hope?" said Kaneesha.

"What's that?" asked Hannah, gathering her hair together at the nape of her neck and putting it into a blue denim scrunchee.

"It's what you need," said Kaneesha.

"Where do you get it, and do they have any left?" asked Hannah, wide-eyed.

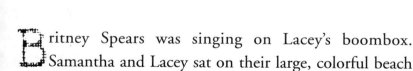

ritney Spears was singing on Lacey's boombox. Samantha and Lacey sat on their large, colorful beach towels, each with a bottle of suntan lotion beside them. There was a cooler at Lacey's feet. Though few people had braved the ocean's chilly temperature on this day at the end of June, there was much activity around the girls. A volleyball game was in full swing about a quarter of a mile down the beach, and several families in varying numbers and combinations were throwing Frisbees.

Samantha was wearing her zebra-striped biker shorts and a sleeveless white T-shirt. She refused to be out in public in a bathing suit. Her toenails were neon orange, and the frames of her sunglasses were bright green.

Lacey had on her new black bikini and oversized, tortoise-shell sunglasses. She had untied the straps of the top of the suit so that her tan would be as seamless as possible. She took a bottle of blue nail enamel out of her tote bag and shook it.

Samantha shielded her eyes from the sun with her forearm.

"So," said Lacey, unscrewing the cap of the bottle, "are you still seeing that Gale Holland person?"

"Yes," said Samantha. "I have no choice about it, but I'm not talking much." She lied. She was talking more than she ever expected to.

"Really, Sam," remarked Lacey, working on her third nail. "I don't see the point of going if you're not going to talk. Why don't you talk to learn stuff? You don't have to change the way you're eating or anything. What are you afraid of?" She fanned out her fingers, examining her nails.

There was a breeze that would dry them quickly. She shook her hand back and forth, waving it in the air.

"If you're so smart, why don't *you* talk to Gale?" said Samantha, only half teasing.

Lacey was blowing on the nails of her other hand, frowning at them, scrutinizing the smooth surfaces for grains of sand that might have stuck there. "Why should I go see her?" asked Lacey. "I don't have any emotional problems. My mother is certainly not on my case about anything."

Samantha turned over onto her stomach and rested her chin on her arms. The volleyball game had broken up and three of the boys were heading for the girls.

One of the boys said, "Hey, Lace, you're looking flatter and flatter, I notice."

"Yeah, well, don't flatter me," answered Lacey, without missing a beat.

Samantha envied Lacey's ability to think fast.

Another boy said, "Hey, Samantha, where's your bathing suit?"

Samantha felt a surge of fear when she heard her name and the words *bathing suit* in the same sentence, but she liked being noticed for her differentness. If a boy told her she looked good, it would mean good by his standards, not by her own. His were the standards that admired the poster of Cindy Crawford, with all that flesh hanging off her.

Samantha was reassured when boys taunted her.

She was looking at the water with her chin propped on her forearms when she saw Brian pass by with Marica Salter. She thought she would die. She felt a lurching in her stomach when she saw Brian with his arm around Marica's shoulders. He was wearing that blue swimsuit, the one that was the same color as his eyes, and Marica had on a black one-piece. She was Samantha's size, petite with a long neck and graceful arms and legs, but with more flesh than Samantha would ever be comfortable having herself.

Samantha couldn't stay in one place for another minute. She thought she was going to be sick. She jumped up suddenly and said, "Lace, we've got to go." She quickly gathered her things, spraying sand onto Lacey's manicure as she reached hastily for her pink beach towel and yellow espadrilles.

The phone was ringing when Gale arrived in her office on Monday morning, and she got to it just before the machine picked up. "Gale Holland," she said breathlessly, dropping the books she was carrying onto the desk.

"Gale? This is Michael McIntyre."

"Oh, hi," said Gale, sitting down at the desk and picking up a pen. "I'm a bit breathless. Excuse me. I ran up the stairs."

"Do you have a minute?" he asked. "I'm not interrupting anything?"

"Not at all. What can I do for you?" she said. She had never heard Phoebe's father's voice, and she was surprised at how gruff he sounded. She had pictured a delicate person when she imagined Phoebe's father, someone who looked like the famous photographer Richard Avedon. This man sounded more like a large army sergeant.

"Well, I understand Phoebe's been coming to see you and, frankly, she doesn't seem to have lost any weight. What am I paying you for if she isn't losing any weight? She works with me over here at the studio, you know, and I really need for her to look a little better, if you know what I mean."

Gale hesitated, momentarily speechless. "Go on," she said.

"Well, I need her to look more fit, you know, a little glamorous. Thinner is what I mean."

"Why?" asked Gale.

"Because of my business, you know," he replied.

"What if you were in a different sort of business?" inquired Gale. "Would you feel any different about Phoebe then?"

"Uh, well, I don't know," said Michael McIntyre. "Anyway, I wanted to know why she hasn't lost any weight yet. Isn't she doing her homework or whatever it is you do with her?"

"Well," said Gale, "this is a gradual, slow process. All you need to know, I think, is that everything is going along just as it should." She hesitated.

When Phoebe's father hadn't replied, she added, "It sounds as though you're having a hard time with this, though."

"Uh, no," said Phoebe's father. "I'm okay. Thanks," and he hung up.

Gale placed the fallen books on a shelf and looked over some papers on her desk while waiting for her first client of the day.

The phone rang again. "Gale? McIntyre again. Look, I just want you to know that I didn't mean what I said before about Phoebe needing to look better. I love the kid, I really do. It's just that I feel for her, you know?"

"Yes," said Gale, with relief, "I know."

* * *

Phoebe went to work on Monday morning with a happy feeling in her heart. She was still fat. She was counting her grams, but she was still big. Her fat was not going to just melt away because she was counting grams, or because she had another appointment with Gale, or because she enjoyed being in group, but she felt happy anyway. Gale said it was because she was taking an action.

When Phoebe got to the studio at 8:45, her father was already there, setting up lights and talking on the phone at the same time. He always did a few things at once, and could never wait for his assistants to get there. He was so impatient. He hung up the phone and looked at his watch.

"Morning, Dad," she said. "What's the good word?"

"The good word, little girl, is that I'm proud of you," announced her father.

Phoebe nearly dropped her bag containing her low-fat lunch. "What?" she asked. She had never heard anything like this from her father before.

"I'm just proud of you, girl," he repeated. He abandoned his lighting project and came to hug her.

Phoebe began to feel teary. Something swelled in her chest, her throat. He had never expressed this much warmth toward her in her entire life.

After work, she went to The Express around the corner.

Their clothes sometimes worked for her if they were baggy enough. Although jeans in their largest size were almost right, a skirt or wide-legged pants would work better if they had elastic waistbands. That day, she got a floaty, navy-blue chiffon skirt with tiny rosebuds printed all over it, and a navy-blue T-shirt with a V-neck and three-quarter–length sleeves. She kept picturing Daryl talking to her when she wore these clothes, the floaty skirt wafting in the breeze.

On the way home, she passed the chocolate shop without even noticing it.

* * *

Samantha looked sullen when Gale greeted her in the waiting room on Monday afternoon, and she kept her eyes in her lap after she'd sat down opposite Gale in the blue brocade armchair, facing the huge painting of grapes.

"How are you doing?" asked Gale.

"Fine," replied Samantha, not looking up.

Gale noticed how Samantha's cuticles had been chewed ragged, how she was tapping her right foot on the carpet— fast little taps—as though she was trying to speed up time.

"What is your foot trying to say?" asked Gale.

"My foot?" answered Samantha. She stopped tapping. "Nothing."

"It's beating out a message in Morse code," said Gale. "What's it saying?"

"It's saying it wants to get out of here, along with the rest of me," said Samantha.

"Where does it want to go?" asked Gale.

"Away." Samantha looked at her watch. It was so quiet in the neighborhood that Samantha could hear the clock ticking, a bird chirping.

"You know," said Gale, "you could come to group here, and then you wouldn't have to sit here all alone with me. At least in group there'd be other people in the room to take the focus off you."

That sounds like an improvement over this, thought Samantha. She looked at the wall behind Gale's desk. Framed certificates were interspersed with small prints of fruits and flowers. She recognized one of the prints from an art class she'd taken one summer. She used to love to draw, and the teacher had said she had talent.

She felt vaguely anxious when she thought about that summer. She remembered feeling happy then. She couldn't figure out what had changed. She hadn't been happy for a single minute since then.

"I have several groups," continued Gale. "The one I think might work best for you is the one that meets Tuesday at 6:00."

"Fine," said Samantha, as she began to gather her book bag.

"Where are you going?" said Gale.

"Well, if I'm coming to group, I'm not sitting here now," she said.

Gale watched as she held onto a chair in the waiting room for support as she walked toward the front door.

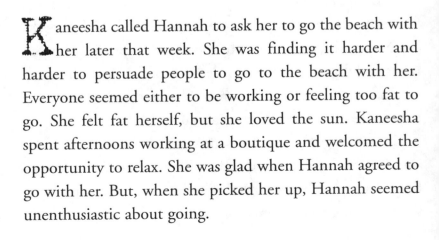

Kaneesha called Hannah to ask her to go the beach with her later that week. She was finding it harder and harder to persuade people to go to the beach with her. Everyone seemed either to be working or feeling too fat to go. She felt fat herself, but she loved the sun. Kaneesha spent afternoons working at a boutique and welcomed the opportunity to relax. She was glad when Hannah agreed to go with her. But, when she picked her up, Hannah seemed unenthusiastic about going.

"What's wrong with you?" asked Kaneesha, as Hannah settled into the passenger seat and put her large, red beach bag on her lap.

"I don't know," sighed Hannah. "I guess I feel nervous about going to the beach. I don't know."

She did know. She had tried to throw up that morning (breakfast had been three bagels with a quarter of a pound of butter and two bowls of oatmeal with cinnamon and raisins) and hadn't been able to. Only blood came up. Her throat felt raw, and she knew she would have to seek help soon. She hoped the bleeding would not occur again, but she didn't know what to do about it. When she swallowed, she tasted that salty blood flavor.

"I don't know," Hannah repeated, looking out the window at the suburban houses with their neat lawns, as well-kept as cemetery plots. She felt as though her life was coming to an end.

The beach was crowded with women of all ages. Hannah spent her time looking at them, assessing their weights, scrutinizing their legs for spidery veins, cellulite and loose flesh, making judgments and pronouncing sentences. *More exercise for that one, no more fat for this one. Ugh, she's eating a hot dog—with those thighs, how could she?* She hardly noticed the many young men looking admiringly at her.

Hannah's one-piece red suit showed off the length of her

legs. But after her big breakfast, over the suit she was wearing a white T-shirt that covered her distended stomach.

Kaneesha's white bikini seemed to fit her perfectly. She ate a hot dog during the afternoon. Hannah ate some applesauce she'd brought. It soothed her throat. Then she drank a half-liter of Diet Coke, which she shared with Kaneesha.

Kaneesha was reading a book called *Twenty-Five Ways to Thinner Thighs.* She finished it in an hour and then leafed through the pages of *Vogue,* studying every detail of the models on the colorful pages.

Hannah suddenly realized she was crazy, crazy to be so concerned about food and weight. She was killing herself. She was killing herself just as her mother had killed herself without knowing that she was doing it.

"I'm going to the ladies' room," said Hannah as she took her bag and walked to the phone.

She left a message on Gale's voice mail, saying she wanted Gale to call her as soon as she could. "I realize it's Sunday," said Hannah into the phone as girls in colorful swimsuits came in and out of the little building that housed the bathrooms, "but I'd appreciate it if you'd call me as soon as you can after I get back. I'll be home in an hour and a half. It's 12:30 now. Thanks."

Then she joined Kaneesha. A copy of *Fitness* magazine was at her feet, the cover showing a photograph of a thin girl in a bikini, her muscles long and lean. Hannah didn't want to look at the photo or at any of the young women at the beach. She felt fat and terribly tired and old.

"I'm going to leave, okay?" she said. "I'll grab the bus back."

"What's wrong? There's still a lot of sun left," said Kaneesha.

"I don't feel very well," said Hannah, which wasn't a lie. She felt weak and headachy, and didn't want to be with anyone.

Hannah left Kaneesha on the beach and waited anxiously for the bus. Maybe Gale had called her back already. Maybe she'd missed her call.

Arlette got on, taking a seat beside Hannah. "Where are you coming from?" asked Arlette.

"From the beach," said Hannah. "How 'bout you?"

"I'm working at Peretti," replied Arlette. "I'm on a lunch break."

"Is that the boutique with the gold-lamé T-shirts?" asked Hannah.

"Yes. So, do you hate those as much as I do?"

"Yes," said Hannah, though actually she loved those gold T-shirts. Except for her dazzling figure, Arlette was not beautiful, Hannah thought. Her features were not wonderful. Her nose was too softly defined and a bit wide for her narrow, oval face. Her lips were a bit too full, but she had a pleasing space between her two front teeth and when she smiled her face was transformed into a light source.

She smiled dazzlingly at Hannah as she got off the bus, and the feelings that arose in Hannah made her very tense. There was only one thing Hannah could think of doing to protect herself from those feelings.

Hannah's phone rang just as she was getting into the house.

"Hannah?" said a familiar voice. "This is Gale Holland."

"I was so upset. Thank you so much for calling me back."

"Of course I called back," said Gale. "What can I do for you?"

Hannah didn't know what to say next. She felt relieved to be off the beach, away from Kaneesha, away from Arlette, but she didn't know what Gale could do for her. "Maybe I should make an appointment," said Hannah.

"Let's do that," said Gale. "Let's also discuss the idea of you joining my group."

"When is it?" asked Hannah anxiously.

"Tuesdays at 6:00. Can you make it?"

❈ ❈ ❈

Phoebe returned from the photo lab with the latest slides of the morning shoot. A model smoking a cigarette sat in a canoe, looking exuberant, as though she was inhaling pure, clean oxygen instead of toxic, life-destroying smoke.

Her father's assistants were setting up the lunch for the crew, an assortment of fancy Italian dishes: penne with pesto, grilled eggplant glistening with olive oil and balsamic vinegar, sausages and peppers, seafood salad, mixed greens and crusty breads. Phoebe saw nothing in this array that would satisfy her low-fat requirement. The seafood salad would have worked, but it appeared to be swimming in oil.

"Hi, Phoebe," said Jacqueline, her father's newest assistant, who was tall and slender, with cropped black hair.

In contrast to the models, who looked so plain and unremarkable when they arrived in the morning until several hours of primping and fussing and fluffing by two or three people turned them into the beauties everyone admired, Jacqueline always looked fantastic in her jeans and T-shirts, without any makeup at all. She had a scrubbed, sparkly aura that Phoebe envied more than the professional gloss of the models.

"You look great, Phoebe," remarked Jacqueline, as she helped herself to the seafood salad, carefully picking around the squid, which she said reminded her of rubber bands.

Phoebe's father had his back to them. He was talking to the stylist about the clothes the model would be wearing in the afternoon: a white chiffon evening dress, accented with sapphire jewelry.

Phoebe took a plate, looked at the food spread attractively on the table and helped herself to a slice of eggplant, some shrimp and scallops from the seafood salad, some greens and a small hunk of bread. Her father turned around just as she was lifting a forkful of eggplant to her lips.

"What are you doing?" he shouted at Phoebe. He had a tone of horror, as though she were preparing to stab herself with a large knife.

"What do you mean?" said Phoebe.

"I mean, what are you eating?"

The entire crew had turned to observe the proceedings.

"Lunch," she said simply.

"It's so fattening!"

The crew was watching Phoebe's humiliation. Jacqueline stared open-mouthed at Phoebe's father while the rest of the staff stared at Phoebe, her fork poised with the eggplant on it.

Her face felt so hot, and drops of perspiration had collected on her forehead. She put down her fork, placed the plate on the table and fled. She could hardly breathe. She stopped, breathed deeply and then walked toward Second Avenue, staring at the people crossing the street, the shop windows, the bus discharging passengers, without seeing.

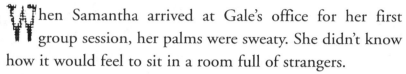

When Samantha arrived at Gale's office for her first group session, her palms were sweaty. She didn't know how it would feel to sit in a room full of strangers.

When she had been in the waiting room for a few minutes, Billy came in. *Oh, great,* thought Samantha. *Fat people and me.*

"Hi," said Billy in a friendly way. "I'm Billy. Are you the new group person?"

"I guess so," answered Samantha. "I guess that's what I am, the new person." *But what a fool I sound like,* she told herself.

"Well, welcome," said Billy. "It's a good group."

"What's good about it?" asked Samantha doubtfully.

"Don't know. It just feels good to be sitting in it for some reason. I thought I'd hate it at first," explained Billy, "but now I look forward to coming."

Sure, you look forward to it, reasoned Samantha, *you would enjoy anything, even being a great, huge blob.* Her usual litany of criticism emerged like a song she couldn't get out of her mind. She judged others harshly, but judged herself with the least mercy of all.

When Scott came in, Samantha was amazed. His slender, movie-star good looks startled her. He looked like Matt Dillon, in fact. She was puzzled about what he was doing in this group. *Surely, he doesn't throw up. How disgusting! Or maybe he cuts himself,* thought Samantha. *But how can I think that's disgusting when that's what I do myself?*

"Hi," said Scott, smiling as he extended his hand to Samantha. "I'm Scott. Who are you?"

"I'm Samantha," she said shyly, feeling her face flush. She felt embarrassed about shaking his hand because her palms were so clammy.

He didn't seem to notice. He smiled. "Welcome."

Just as he said this, Gale stuck her head out of her office and said, "Come in, gang." They all trooped into the office.

As they were seating themselves in the wing chairs in front of the fireplace, Phoebe arrived, looking very upset. She was breathing rapidly, having run down the street to get there on time.

"What happened to you?" asked Billy.

Phoebe didn't know what to say. She had spent the afternoon walking around the city, not knowing where she was going. When she realized she had to get to the railroad station to catch her train, she raced over there, just making the 5:08. She'd had to stand all the way to Gale's stop, and then run four long blocks to get to Gale's office. She couldn't imagine ever talking to her father again or even looking at him. She couldn't possibly imagine going back to the studio to work.

Phoebe, disoriented and vague, couldn't focus. The group waited for her to say something.

Her eyes filled with tears. Her pretty face flushed with anger. Phoebe described how her father had humiliated her. She felt grateful when Scott said, "Boy, Phoebe, you must be so angry."

"Phoebe—how awful." It was Samantha, who was amazed to hear her own voice speaking up in group.

Phoebe sniffed away her tears as Billy handed her the box of pink tissues from the top of the window seat.

"Well," said Gale, "we have a new member tonight, but let's jump right in, and we'll do introductions later. Who identifies with Phoebe?"

Samantha found herself raising her hand. As soon as she did, she felt regret.

"How do you identify, Samantha?" asked Gale.

"Well," she began reluctantly, "my mother nags me about eating all the time and tells me how thin I look, and I just can't stand it. It's like she's underneath my skin or something, and I feel like I just want to cut her out of there."

"Did you hear what you just said, Samantha, about cutting her out?" asked Gale.

"Yes," said Samantha thoughtfully.

"Maybe we could talk about that another time," suggested Gale.

"Okay," agreed Samantha.

"Phoebe, what are you going to do?" asked Billy, always the practical one. "You do work there after all."

"What about an unsent letter?" suggested Faye.

"What's that?" asked Phoebe.

"What you do is write a letter telling the person how what they did made you feel," said Faye, "and you tell them what you need. I wrote one of those to my mother and it was amazing how relieved I felt, how clear. I even started feeling a little like forgiving her, and I never, ever thought I could feel that way, ever. Of course I never sent the letter because my mother died when I was in my teens. She killed herself."

Phoebe was horrified. "How did she do it?"

"With cocaine," said Faye.

"How awful!" exclaimed Phoebe.

"But this is about you," Faye reminded her.

Phoebe sighed. She deliberated. "I want to give him the letter," she said firmly, "and I want to do it before the group meets again."

"Why don't you call me and read it to me?" suggested Faye.

"I want to hear it, too," said Scott.

"Me, too," Billy added.

"I'm a little nervous," said Phoebe, "about his reaction."

"Why don't we do a role-play, Phoebe?" suggested Gale. "Pick someone in the room to be your dad and tell him how his behavior today made you feel. Then maybe you'll be a bit more confident. Rehearsals always help."

Phoebe looked around the room. Her gaze settled upon Samantha. She felt something in her wanting to choose Samantha.

"Samantha," she said.

Samantha had a sinking feeling. "Me?" she said.

"Do you mind?" asked Gale. "You don't have to do it."

"I mind," continued Samantha, "but I will do it."

"Okay," continued Gale. "Phoebe and Samantha, move your chairs closer together and face each other. Okay, Phoebe, go."

Phoebe thought for a minute. "When you said, 'What are you eating?' today, I felt so humiliated. I wanted to drop down into the floor, and afterwards I wanted to smack you and scream at you." Tears filled her eyes again.

"I was only being helpful," said Samantha as Phoebe's dad. "I want you to be happy and pretty."

Samantha was amazed at the ease with which she had become a part of the group.

"I am happy and pretty already," insisted Phoebe, surprising herself with this information.

Samantha was stumped. What could she say? *No, you aren't?* How could she tell her own daughter that she wasn't happy, wasn't pretty? "Well," Samantha said finally, "I just thought you would feel better about yourself if you would lose some weight."

"Well, I was already feeling good about myself, and now I feel disgusting. I need for you to let me be me!"

Samantha was completely stumped then. There was nothing she could do now as Phoebe's father but apologize, and she didn't want to. She just wanted to be right, no matter what, even if she was wrong.

"How do you feel right now, Samantha, as Phoebe's dad?" asked Gale.

"I feel like the only thing left for me to do is apologize, but I don't want to," said Samantha.

"Hah!" said Phoebe. "You were wrong, you know you were! You hurt me so much. I don't know if I can ever forgive you!"

Again Samantha was silent.

"Do you think your father would be silent at this point?" asked Scott.

"I don't know," said Phoebe. "He hates being wrong, absolutely hates it. I don't think I've ever heard him apologize for anything. I think if I wrote down a few things, too, I would feel better," said Phoebe.

She was feeling comforted by the group. Was she missing this feeling all the time in her real life? Was this the way life was supposed to feel? It made her sad to have missed out.

Samantha was uncomfortable sitting in the middle of the room. Her foot began to shake back and forth. Gale noticed and said, "Do you want to run away, Samantha?"

"I guess so," admitted Samantha.

"Thanks," said Phoebe. "You said just the things my father would have."

After Samantha had introduced herself to the group members and had explained that she had come to therapy in the first place because she would otherwise have been put into a hospital, group was over. The time had gone by really quickly. Samantha was angry at herself for having enjoyed it.

When Samantha arrived home that night, she decided to go to bed without vacuuming her room, even though she was afraid that if she neglected it just this once she might never clean her room again and it would be a shambles, that she would be consumed by fatness and dust.

* * *

Hannah finished her studying for the day and sighed. She felt like a fool for calling Gale. She didn't know how she was going to get herself to group, the thought of which terrified her, but, if she didn't do something, how could she go on? How could she continue to eat the way she did and not be able to throw up?

She took a photo album from one of the shelves in her room, the album with the blue, flowery print on the cover, and looked at the picture of her mother, the one that had been taken on the beach the year before she died.

She was on a blanket with her knitting beside her, and she was smiling at Hannah's aunt, who was holding the camera. Her mother had been knitting a yellow sweater for Hannah, a turtleneck with cable stitches, which she still had. Her mother's thin legs and bony shoulders made her look frail, especially in the bright, penetrating sunlight.

She looked happy with herself in the picture, but Hannah knew better. She knew her mother hated herself. Her mother had admitted this to Hannah often. *Appearances certainly can be deceiving,* thought Hannah.

* * *

Jessica had found a boyfriend, someone her mother's friend, Keith, had brought around one night, someone who had been arrested once for possession of cocaine, someone older.

She was using more caffeine now, drinking stronger coffee in the morning, and using herbal stimulants to give her energy. She was wearing more makeup because she had gotten so tired-looking, even with her tan.

Her boyfriend thought going to the beach was boring, so she seldom went anymore. He had a BMW convertible, which Jessica borrowed, so she never took the bus anymore. Sometimes she and her mother would double-date. Jessica's boyfriend was almost as old as her mother. His name was Steve, and he had the same interests as Keith—cars, boats, gambling and money.

* * *

Phoebe gripped the doorknob so tightly that her knuckles were white as she pushed open the front door of her house. She had no idea what she was going to say to her father, in spite of the rehearsal she had just had in group. She knew this would be a good time to talk with him since her mother was out playing bridge.

The hallway just inside the door and the kitchen beyond were dimly lit. In the large family room beyond the kitchen, Phoebe could see the back of her father's head framed by the light from the TV flickering in eerie colors. It was a cool, breezy evening, and Phoebe could smell the aroma of a neighbor's barbecue.

Her thoughts were muddled. Everything was changing fast, and she didn't know what life was going to feel like on the other side of the change.

She took off her green backpack and left it on the floor leaning up against the hall table where the day's mail sat in a neat stack. She walked through the kitchen and into the family room, where her father sat before the giant screen, flipping channels. He got hypnotized in front of the TV, Phoebe reminded herself. It didn't matter what he was watching; he seemed partially absent. She didn't want to interrupt him in the midst of something he might be absorbed by. Timing was important.

"Hi," she said. She tried to make her tone casual.

He didn't look away from the screen, didn't even look at her. "Hi," he answered distractedly.

Phoebe waited for him to turn to look at her, to acknowledge her.

Now she was really mad. Here she was, standing in the same room with him, and he hadn't even looked up.

"Why can't you even look at me when I come into a room?" she shouted, choking back tears, years of memories. "How can you not even look up? It's basic courtesy. You wouldn't think of not looking up if a client came into the studio and said hi. I just hate you! I hate you!"

She ran out of the house and into the street.

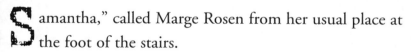

Samantha," called Marge Rosen from her usual place at the foot of the stairs.

Samantha was listening to Smashing Pumpkins beyond the whir of the vacuum cleaner. She was thinking about everything she'd heard in group, everything she'd said, and she had been thinking about these things for three days. The whole experience made her so agitated that the only way she could calm herself was to reorganize her closets and drawers and clean her already-spotless room. She even vacuumed the carpet in the hall and the one in her sister's room, although that was always such a mess there was hardly any rug visible under all the clothes. She didn't turn off the vacuum cleaner when she heard her mother call.

"Samantha," repeated her mother, "can I come in and talk with you?"

Samantha, irritated, turned off the music and the vacuum cleaner and went to the door. "No, I'll come out." She didn't like having her mother in her room. It was her private place. Whenever someone came in, she felt she had to clean it all over again. She opened her door and found her mother standing at the threshold, holding a hairbrush.

"Remember? When you were a little girl, I used to brush your hair. I was thinking about that today. I was going through the photo albums, and I found a picture of me braiding your hair. Would you let me braid it now? We could talk. You've always admired those French braids Alexa's mom does for her."

"Well," said Samantha, "I don't mind if you braid my hair, but I don't feel like talking right now." It was hard for Samantha to sound accommodating and cold in the same sentence. She felt awkward, horrified to be standing so close to her mother, to have said yes to something. She felt so sad.

"Could we do this downstairs," said Samantha, making it an assertion instead of a question.

They walked downstairs, Samantha following behind her mother. In the living room, the orderliness of the furniture seemed to say, "Don't touch me; I'm perfect; you'll spoil me." Samantha's mother sat on one of the beige armchairs. Samantha sat at the far end of a large matching sofa. The room always reminded Samantha of Christmas, which was one of the few times the family used the living room.

"I wondered how you were doing with Gale," said her mother, holding the hairbrush awkwardly in her lap.

"Okay, I guess. I'm going, aren't I? That's all I agreed to do."

Samantha sounded more sullen than she had intended. She and her mother didn't have a habitual tone in which they conversed. They never did converse anymore. Samantha didn't want to seem too friendly. Her mother might get into the habit of having more talks with her.

"I just wondered if . . . well . . . if it was helping," said her mother, picking imaginary lint off the black linen of her slacks.

"Helping what?" said Samantha.

Her mother looked down at the brush in her lap.

Samantha began to feel sorry for her. It was not a familiar feeling, but it was a strong one, and it made her want to take care of her mother.

"You can brush my hair if you want to now," said Samantha, coming to sit closer. There was no harm in having her mother brush her hair. It wasn't fattening.

Samantha's mother looked up, startled, and then moved closer to Samantha. Samantha turned her back so that her mother could brush her long, straight, blond hair.

"You've always had such beautiful hair," said her mother.

*　*　*

Heat and humidity covered Jessica with a film of perspiration. She was so weak that morning that she couldn't face getting dressed. Even the effort of lifting her arms to slip a T-shirt over her head seemed far too strenuous, and she decided to stay in her bathrobe all day. It seemed as though every bone and muscle in her body ached. She loved the gray, paisley silk robe that Matthew and her mother had given her last Christmas. It was easy to get into and felt so cool against her skin.

As she walked downstairs, holding tightly to the banister, she noticed her heartbeat becoming uneven, just for a second or two. She breathed deeply and evenly and it stabilized, but she felt lightheaded and her stomach ached.

I need a cup of strong coffee, she thought, *and some laxatives.* She hadn't exercised in four whole days and decided that, if she didn't have the energy to exercise, she would have to take some laxatives to make herself feel clean, emptied out inside, to make her stomach perfectly flat. Also, she hated her thighs. No matter how little she ate, they never looked thin enough to her. She hated the way they spread out sideways when she sat down and wondered if other people's thighs did that.

After Matthew got home from day camp, she spent the afternoon playing video games with him and helping him build a Lego movie theater. She had her usual ration of two slices of dry toast and two liters of Diet Coke that day, and tried not to let Matthew notice how weak she was.

Was blood really connective tissue? It was hard for Hannah to think of blood as connective. Biology was what connected her to her mother. Blood was, too. Blood was connective. It traveled around, made connections, delivered nutrients and oxygen, took away metabolic residue. Hannah breathed easily, visualizing the path that oxygen took in the body. She was understanding biology better.

Miraculously, her father had helped her understand blood pressure. He had been trained as a paramedic, though he'd never actually worked as one, and he knew lots of useful stuff if you were trying to pass biology. He'd taken her to dinner, and then they'd sat on her bed and he'd explained how blood pressure was related to kidneys. The dinner was at her favorite Italian restaurant, Mamma Mia. She felt blimpy afterwards, but didn't even try to throw up the manicotti. She didn't know why. She just hadn't felt the need.

The sound of the rain on the roof, the warmth of the summer night, the comforting presence of her father in the house made her feel safe, complete. *I'm having a rare moment,* observed Hannah, *a rare happy moment.* It unsettled her. A few minutes later, she was eating cookie-crunch ice cream.

* * *

Phoebe decided after having walked around for about half an hour that she had to go back into her house to confront her father more calmly. After all, she had a job with him, and they had to live together, for the moment anyway. Suddenly, she couldn't wait to go away to college where she would be free. She walked back to her house, up the paved path between the two sections of the front lawn and through the large, white front door.

Her father was still glassy-eyed, watching TV. The image on the screen was of a dark-haired beauty in a leotard on a treadmill. Phoebe dimly remembered that it was a commercial her father had shot before she started her summer at the studio. When he heard someone come in, he turned off the TV and came into the hall, looking at her with a blank expression.

"What's up? Are you having your period or something?" he asked.

That was another maddening thing. Whenever anything seemed to be the matter with either Phoebe or her mother, her father always decided to blame it on their periods. It was as though nothing otherwise could be wrong between them.

"No," she said, then ran upstairs to her room. She sat on her bed and looked around.

The painting of a pink rose in a crystal vase was hanging above her bed. Her father had given it to her for her twelfth birthday, saying, "It's time you had some real art in your room, Phoebe. It's very important to look at art, to appreciate handmade things. You may not appreciate this right now, but you will thank me later. I think your posters are fine, but you need a real painting to look at."

She looked at the musical jewelry box on her dressing table, the one her father had bought her when she was thirteen. It was wood and in the shape of a Swiss chalet with tiny, carved wooden flowers all around it in little window boxes. The flowers were painted all the colors of the rainbow. When you opened the roof of the chalet, there was a plastic ballerina in a white tulle tutu going around and around on a spring to the "Blue Danube" waltz.

She had to take deep breaths to calm herself down before she had the composure to walk downstairs to speak to him. When she finally did go downstairs, she pretended she was in group and the remarks she was making to her father were being made to Samantha. She waited for him to react defensively, the way he always did. He did.

"I'm just concerned for your happiness," he said when she'd finished. "It's you I'm thinking of."

"Well," said Phoebe, "that can't possibly be true because if you really were concerned about me, you wouldn't be so cruel. You wouldn't have humiliated me in front of all those people today at the studio."

Her father didn't say, "You're right, I'm so sorry," but he moved toward her and took her into his arms and held her.

Phoebe wished he had said, "You're right, Phoebe, I'm so sorry I did that to you," but she let herself be held.

Jessica opened her eyes after a sleepless night and felt a hundred years old. All her bones, even her teeth, ached. Her eyes burned, and her ears were ringing. She had been drinking a dozen cups of coffee a day—strong coffee—and had been taking laxatives for six days in a row. She'd started smoking more, too, but when she placed her hand over her stomach it was perfectly flat. This made everything worth it.

The day stretched before her. Phoebe worked at the studio all day. Jessica didn't have the energy to get out of bed anyway, much less go anywhere to see friends. She knew that right away. She didn't have the energy to take Matt to the movies when he got home from day camp. She had the whole day to herself and thought she might do some sewing. She had an idea for a pair of Lycra overalls. She enjoyed making clothes, but hadn't done any sewing for a long time.

She swung her legs over and let them dangle off the side of the bed, sitting up. Black spots sprang up behind her eyes. Lights flashed there, as though a police car had moved into her head, its lights revolving around and around.

Closing her eyes didn't make them go away. She tried standing, holding onto the headboard for support, steadying herself. Then she reached for the robe at the foot of the bed, pulling it on. It was so chilly. It was the first of August, and she was so cold. When she tied the robe snugly around her tiny waist, she felt dizzy and grabbed the side of the bureau for support as she moved toward the door.

❀ ❀ ❀

Samantha was in the waiting room when Hannah arrived for her first session in the Tuesday night group.

"Hi," said Samantha, with a brightness that surprised herself. "I'm Samantha."

"I'm Hannah." Her mouth was dry. Her hands, freezing.

When it came time for Hannah to introduce herself to the group, she smiled and said shyly, "Hi, I'm Hannah, and I get sick."

"You get sick?" said Faye. "What do you mean?"

"You know," answered Hannah, "I get sick."

"You mean you throw up," said Scott.

"Yes."

"Well, why didn't you say so?" said Scott. "It's not such a big deal that you can't say it. It's not a dirty word."

"Well, it is disgusting," replied Hannah softly.

"Did you come because you want to stop throwing up?" asked Scott.

"I came because I want to stop bleeding when I do it." Hannah was still unable to say the offending words.

"Have you seen a doctor?" asked Gale.

"No," said Hannah. "I don't want to. I just want the bleeding to stop."

"I didn't know you'd been bleeding," said Gale.

"I have been," she said. There. Now she'd said it out loud in a room full of people. She felt relieved.

"Will you commit to making an appointment with a doctor this week?" said Gale. "I can recommend a doctor if you don't have one you're comfortable with. I can't continue to see you unless you see a doctor."

"I don't know," said Hannah.

"Well, I can't work with you if you're in medical danger and not in a doctor's care," explained Gale.

Good, thought Hannah, *don't see me then.*

"So, I'll give you the name of a doctor after the session." Then Gale said, "So, group, any hot news bulletins?"

Phoebe said, "I talked to my father. It didn't go that well at first, but it's okay now. Now I want to talk to my mom."

Phoebe thought about her mother as she let herself into the house that evening. Her mother was at the mall, starting her Christmas shopping, and Phoebe smiled, thinking about her mother's habit of starting her Christmas shopping in August.

"Hi," said Phoebe, as Molly McIntyre came into the kitchen less than five minutes behind Phoebe. "Did you get some good stuff?"

Molly set several shopping bags down on the floor. "Yep," she said, "but they can't be opened until Christmas."

Molly walked to the stove to boil some water for tea and noticed the message light on the answering machine was blinking. She pressed the listen button, and the tape rewound with its familiar chirping sound. Then it beeped and on came the voice of Jessica's mother, Adrianne Blaine.

Adrianne sounded hoarse, distressed, as though she'd been crying. "Phoebe, come see me right away. This is Adrianne. Something awful has happened, something really, really awful. It's Jessica. I don't want to tell you on the phone."

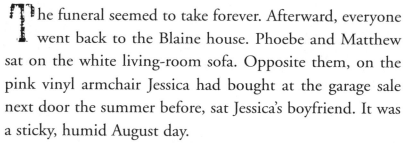

The funeral seemed to take forever. Afterward, everyone went back to the Blaine house. Phoebe and Matthew sat on the white living-room sofa. Opposite them, on the pink vinyl armchair Jessica had bought at the garage sale next door the summer before, sat Jessica's boyfriend. It was a sticky, humid August day.

Matthew was toughing it out, sitting very stiffly, hardly moving even his eyes. His shorts were navy blue, and they were new and bright. He rubbed a spot on his bare knee with his thumb, as though it hurt and he was soothing it. His white T-shirt still had creases from having been folded, and the way its short sleeves stood away from his arms made them look like sticks. He wore no shoes, only Jessica's favorite socks, red-and-white–striped ones that were far too big for him. They drooped flaccidly from his toes and bunched up around his ankles.

Phoebe was wearing her navy-blue chiffon skirt with the little pink rosebuds and the navy-blue T-shirt. She watched Jessica's mother crying at the far end of the room, where she sat, her shoulders hunched in an attitude of defeat, surrounded by her family. She looked childlike, her body deflated.

Among her friends who came to pay their respects was a leading man from a TV soap that Adrianne had worked on. He recognized Phoebe from her father's studio. "Your dad helped me get my career started," he said to Phoebe. "Were you a friend of Adrianne's daughter?"

"Yes," said Phoebe sadly. "I was her friend."

Phoebe thought back to when she and Jessica had met. Jessica had moved to Heathbrook just in time to start kindergarten. Phoebe, able to muster compassion for a stranger even at the tender age of five, hardly left Jessica's side that whole first year.

All around them, people whispered and commiserated. There was lots of food on hand. Phoebe was hungry, but didn't feel it was appropriate for her to be eating in Jessica's house for some reason; she felt it would show a lack of respect for Jessica if she ate. She never felt comfortable eating in public places anyway. She was afraid of what people might think: the fat girl eating even more.

Phoebe said, "Matty, do you want to come and sit in my lap?"

"No, thank you," said Matthew politely, his eyes downcast. He crossed his hands in his lap. His long eyelashes fringed the tops of his pale cheeks, and his hair hung limply over his forehead in spiky points.

Phoebe pleated a tissue carefully, methodically. She used

her index finger to space each fold evenly and then pressed the folds into sharp creases on her thigh with her thumb. She recognized several teachers from the high school, the cheerleading coach among them.

She heard the word *anorexia*, and someone said, "First the husband, then the daughter. Poor Adrianne."

The woman behind Phoebe said, "She passed out in her bedroom."

Someone else whispered, "She was on the carpet when Adrianne found her later in the day. Thank God Matthew didn't find her. Adrianne had only gone to an exercise class."

Hannah had come to the Blaines to be with Phoebe, to support her. Hannah heard the word *hospital* and remembered the many months that she and her father would go to the hospital every night after dinner. Those dinners were awful. She and her dad would sit at the table and pretend that things were normal, that Hannah's mother was in the hospital only temporarily. Hannah felt nauseated after eating those dinners.

She'd been feeling good about herself, about her courage in calling Gale. She'd been feeling good about having passed the biology final in summer school.

All at once, she felt horrified at herself, guilty for thinking about biology when a young girl, someone her own age, was dead. But didn't life have to go on? Wasn't it natural for the living to continue to think and hope and plan?

Slowly, a realization gripped Hannah, flowing through her body like an electrical wave. If life could go on, if it was natural for life to go on, maybe it was all right for her to let her own life continue past her mother's.

Phoebe felt exhausted. She could hardly hold up her head.

The funeral had been horribly painful. At least there had been no trip to a cemetery. Jessica had said she wanted to be cremated, that it was the only civilized way to treat yourself after you were dead. Matthew had told Adrianne this news while Adrianne was making funeral arrangements. This topic of what to do with yourself after you had died had been a favorite topic of Matthew's.

The funeral was tearful. The newspaper had sent a reporter who had interviewed Adrianne and some of Jessica's friends. Phoebe hated being interviewed. She felt like a politician at some sort of press conference instead of the friend of a dead sixteen-year-old girl.

I wish this afternoon would end already, thought Phoebe, longing to be alone. Then she noticed what she had been thinking and how strange it was that you waited and waited in such deep anticipation, hoping that time would speed up so that you could get somewhere or do something or know something. But, if time were to really speed up, life would just go by more quickly and all of a sudden it would end, like Jessica's had. Jessica would never know what the future had held for her.

Beside Phoebe there was a table full of food brought by neighbors and friends: covered casseroles and crock pots, trays of sandwiches and cold cuts, dishes of pickles, bowls of nuts and dried fruits.

"Do you want something to eat, Matt?" asked Phoebe.

Matthew was looking tired. He had been sitting up straight, bracing himself against grief far too long.

"I don't want anything to eat," he said. "If Jessica were here, she wouldn't have eaten. I'm not either. I want to be like her."

The next time group met, Phoebe explained that her best friend had died. She cried again for a long time, and every member of the group hugged her.

Hannah said she felt guilty that she hadn't cried when her mom died. *What's wrong with me?* wondered Hannah. *I'm horrible; I deserve to be miserable.*

"What else interests you besides bingeing and purging and feeling miserable, Hannah?" asked Gale.

Hannah looked blankly into space. "I don't know anymore," reflected Hannah. "I used to love playing the guitar and the harmonica. Now I'd have to think about it. Isn't that crazy? I don't even know what interests me."

"You must be interested in clothes," offered Samantha. "You have a really good sense of color." She looked admiringly at Hannah's hot-pink-and-orange–striped rayon miniskirt and red T-shirt.

Hannah felt too large when she was the center of attention. She stammered awkwardly.

"It seems hard for you to accept compliments," observed Gale.

"It's hard being the center of attention. It makes me feel squirmy and embarrassed."

"Samantha," said Gale, "how do you feel about being complimented?"

"I don't know," answered Samantha. "Sometimes I get complimented about my room. It's always very neat."

"Do you ever get complimented for anything else?" asked Gale.

"No," said Samantha, "and I don't want to start now."

Everybody laughed.

That was really funny, thought Samantha. She had made

everyone laugh. It felt so good. Samantha felt tears rising up into her throat, but she quickly swallowed them, forcing them back down.

"Well," said Gale, "how did it feel to have everyone appreciate you?"

"It felt as though I actually might belong somewhere," said Samantha with relief. She sniffled, and Scott handed her a box of tissues. "I felt so lonely the other day," she admitted, blotting at her eyes with the tissue, "that I cut myself. I'm so afraid that you'll be disappointed with me, all of you." She was amazed at herself for having blurted out this secret.

"That you cut yourself? Where?" said Faye.

Samantha was wearing yellow leggings that came to just below her knees. She pulled up the left leg of the stretchy pants and showed the group the cross she had carved just above her knee. It was healing quickly, but it still looked angry around the edges.

"Oh, my God," said Hannah, aghast at the idea that someone she knew had actually done that to her own flesh. "Do you really do that to yourself?"

"Yes," said Samantha, "I do."

"Why?" asked Hannah.

"When I do it, it's because I feel I just have to," said Samantha, pulling the pant leg back down over her knee.

The group was silent for a minute. Then Hannah spoke. "Sometimes I feel I want to punish myself. Does it feel like that?"

"Sort of," replied Samantha. "Why do you want to punish yourself?" She wanted to have the focus of attention off herself.

"Because my mother died," said Hannah. "My mother was really, really skinny." She hesitated as though she was forming a picture of her mother in her mind. "And I never said a single word to her about it. I mean, she had cancer and everything, but she was always on a diet, too. And when she was on a diet, I'd always cheer her on, like if she lost two pounds and she was so happy, I'd say, 'Way to go, Mom,' and stuff like that. But I never sat down with her to tell her how I felt about her weight, which was terrible of me. I never told her how I felt about it."

"But you did the best you could," protested Phoebe. "You didn't want to hurt her feelings."

"Exactly," said Hannah, with obvious relief. "I didn't want to hurt her."

"That's how I felt about my father's drinking," reflected Faye.

"It might not have done any good anyway," added Phoebe.

Hannah sighed. She cocked her head to one side. "My

mom and I, we were like friends sort of. When I didn't feel like going to school, she'd write me a note saying I was sick. We'd sit on her bed all day and watch talk shows and soaps and eat popcorn, huge bowls of it. Well, I'd eat it really. She didn't like going out, being with people. She seemed sad all the time. It was as though I was her best friend, except for Rose down the street. Sometimes I wanted to go out, be with girls my age, but I never wanted to leave her. She depended on me. She depended on me and trusted me. I could have helped her."

"Why would your mother have listened to you?" said Faye. "I wouldn't have listened. Samantha doesn't listen to her mother. Nobody listens."

Hannah considered this. The group remained silent.

Gale said, "Samantha, do you want to say anything else about cutting yourself?"

"No," said Samantha, "I don't right now."

The group was silent again.

Phoebe said, "I feel so bad about Jessica. I went to see her at the hospital the first time she collapsed, and I didn't say anything to her. I can't believe I did that. I didn't say anything about her starving."

The group considered this.

"I think I want to say something now, though," said Phoebe to Faye.

"What?" said Faye.

"I want to say, 'Faye, you're so thin, I'm worried about you.'"

Faye looked at her lap.

"I'm worried about you, Faye," repeated Phoebe.

The room was silent.

Faye said finally, "I'm afraid. I'm afraid to eat."

"I know," said Samantha softly.

"Maybe you could get some help, like in a hospital or something," continued Phoebe. "I read about hyperalimentation. They put a tube into you and feed you and—"

"I'd die first," said Faye resolutely.

"That's what Jessica said," remembered Phoebe bitterly.

"Faye," said Hannah, "I need to let you know that, when you say you'd rather die than be fed through a tube, I feel so angry at you, but at the same time I understand that feeling."

Scott said, "Faye, when you keep starving, you're hurting not only yourself but everyone who cares about you."

"Nobody cares about me," said Faye.

"That's not true," said Hannah. "I care about you. Phoebe and Samantha care about you."

"Speak for yourself," said Samantha.

Everyone laughed heartily, including Faye.

Samantha thought, *I can be really funny. I never knew that about myself until now.*

"What about you, Samantha?" asked Gale. "What would you like to say to Faye?"

"I would like to say that she needs to eat more and throw up less, because she does not realize she could die."

"In other words," said Gale, "you think Faye should learn to handle her bulimia more effectively."

"Exactly," said Samantha.

Everyone laughed again.

Samantha was enjoying herself. It scared her.

Phoebe turned to Faye. "Faye," she said, "I know you think I'm disgustingly fat, but I need for you to know that, while I may be disgustingly fat in your eyes, at least I haven't died."

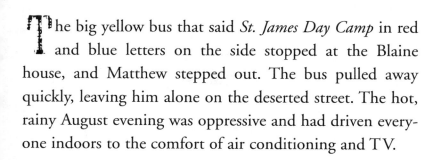

The big yellow bus that said *St. James Day Camp* in red and blue letters on the side stopped at the Blaine house, and Matthew stepped out. The bus pulled away quickly, leaving him alone on the deserted street. The hot, rainy August evening was oppressive and had driven everyone indoors to the comfort of air conditioning and T.V.

As Matthew headed for the house, the toe of his sneaker caught on one of the bricks dividing the pebbled driveway from the grass and he tripped, scraping his knee on the gravel and twisting his knee at the same time. He hobbled across the lawn and let himself into the empty house. It was so quiet he could hear the clock ticking in the screened-in porch and the drip, drip, drip of the kitchen faucet.

A sudden downpour while he was waiting for the bus had left him drenched. He climbed the stairs to his room to change his clothes. Each stair seemed very big and very high, and each step required great effort. He pulled himself up using the banister for support to avoid putting weight on his knee. The soft, furry pandas and elephants looking down at him from the shelves on the walls of his room seemed menacing in the silence. His baby-sitter would be coming soon, he guessed. She was late and should have come already.

The house seemed enormous and cold and scary without Jessica.

* * *

Samantha came into the house after group one night, and her mother's voice greeted her from the kitchen.

"How was group?" her mother asked, not really expecting any more than a mumbled reply.

"It was all right," said Samantha. She walked into the kitchen instead of immediately retreating to her room.

Her mother was emptying the dishwasher. She was surprised that Samantha hadn't raced upstairs as she usually did.

Samantha noticed the lines around her mother's mouth and darkening circles beneath her eyes. She didn't look well, and Samantha felt a sudden surge of sympathy for her.

"The group is all right," she repeated. "There's a really thin girl in it. . . ." She let her voice trail off. She was being too chatty. She had never been like this with her mother.

Marge looked quickly at her from her dishes. She was startled by her daughter's sudden willingness to talk. Samantha did not intend to tell her mother about Jessica dying.

"I've got to get ready," added Samantha hurriedly. "I'm going out with Hannah and Phoebe tonight. They're from group."

"Where are you going?" asked her mother.

"Well, I think we're going to just hang out at Hannah's,"

replied Samantha, who was lying. Actually, they planned to drive around with some boys, friends of Billy's they'd met after group one night.

One of the boys had driven Samantha home while her car was being serviced. His name was Len and he had just graduated, and Samantha thought he was really cute. He listened, too, which in her experience was unusual. They'd talked about therapy because Len had been in therapy, too. He was having trouble figuring out what to do with his anger at his father, who was always criticizing him and said he could never do anything right.

Len was majoring in art and planned to go to the Rhode Island School of Design. His father thought majoring in art was the silliest, most irresponsible thing a man could do. He wanted Len to major in marketing so he could take over his father's fur business. Len didn't even believe people should wear fur.

Len and Billy were going to pick up Samantha, Hannah and Phoebe at Hannah's house. Then, they were going to drive around and then maybe go over to Port Franklin and see what was happening there. Port Franklin was a waterfront town with funky little shops and coffeehouses and ice-cream stands and moonlight on the water.

"Well, try to be home by midnight," said Samantha's mother.

Midnight? thought Samantha. *How can I be home by midnight when they aren't even going to pick us up until 11:00?*

"Oh, I'm not coming home," lied Samantha, gathering her book bag from the counter and slinging it over her shoulder. "I'm going to sleep over at Hannah's." Hannah didn't know this yet, but Samantha would figure out something.

* * *

Phoebe was putting away some of the props that had been used by the cast and crew of the commercial her father was shooting at his studio. It was the end of a long work day. It had begun at dawn in Port Franklin with a sequence that needed a sunrise over water, and it ended at the studio with a difficult shot involving a dog. Animals were always challenging, Phoebe was learning. Last week, a baby ocelot had bitten a model's thigh.

At lunch that day, some of the models were talking about their (imaginary) fat. One of them had been complaining that she'd gained a pound, and Phoebe had said to the assembled group, "A waist is a terrible thing to mind." It had just popped into her head. Everyone laughed heartily, and her father had looked at her with pride.

Now he finished his phone call and approached the corner of the studio in which she was folding a large, black cloth that had been used as a backdrop. Her father studied her with that look that always frightened her. It seemed to her so penetrating and critical, assessing every line. After he had appraised her for a moment, he said, "You're losing weight." Then he turned and went into the reception area to check on the bookings for the next day.

Phoebe was pleased. She really had been working hard on lowering her fat intake and increasing the amount of time she spent exercising.

When her father came back into the studio, he said, "I'm really proud of the effort you're making, sweetheart. You're doing great."

* * *

The August sun slanted into the Blaine kitchen where Matthew sat. It illuminated the green counters and cabinets and the faded pink-and-white wallpaper with the repeating pattern of trellis roses. It highlighted the dark stains where Matthew had thrown his spaghetti when he was just a baby. The sun was so dazzling that Matthew had to squint. He slumped at the kitchen table, his bowl of granola untouched, his banana unpeeled, his hair tousled from sleep.

"I don't like this brand of granola, Mom," he whined. "Jessica always used to get me that other brand with the covered wagon on the box."

Adrianne stood at the counter looking out the window at the neighbor's yard, where white phlox bloomed. Labor Day was fast approaching. There had been some windy days that carried the scent of autumn, when Matthew would be starting second grade. Adrianne had some important decisions to make. She sighed and turned toward him, not having heard what he said, looking at the sun pooling on the table beside his bowl. When Skye was still with them, they'd eaten hundreds of breakfasts at that table, thousands of dinners. Turning back to the window, she picked up the sponge and wiped the counter distractedly.

"Ma!" whined Matthew. "I said I don't like this brand of granola, and this banana isn't ripe enough yet, either. Jessica always—"

Adrianne slammed her hand down on the counter. "I don't want to hear this anymore," she said sharply. "I can't listen to this anymore!"

* * *

I need to say that I'm totally fed up with myself," said Hannah to the group. She was wearing white cutoffs and a white T-shirt that emphasized the bronze brilliance of her late-summer tan. Her toenails, visible beyond the straps of her red sandals, were painted blue, and she wore an anklet of white shells.

"Samantha and I spent last night together. We talked and told each other things about ourselves. We were together for over two hours. Then I came home and binged anyway. Nothing I do seems to help me feel better. I'm afraid of waking up in the morning because I might feel as though I want to eat everything in the house, everything on the block, even, and then of course I'll want to throw it all up. It just goes on and on this way, and I can't stand it anymore. I can't stand waking up and thinking of nothing except food and my body and food and my body. I'd rather just die. I really would. I'd rather be six feet under than go through this for another day. I'm almost seventeen years old. I should be having fun. I don't even know what the word 'fun' means."

"What is fun, anyway?" finished Hannah, more to herself than to the others.

Gale looked around at the members of the group. Tears were running down Samantha's face. "Do you identify with what Hannah is saying, Samantha?" asked Gale softly.

Samantha nodded without speaking.

The group was quiet. Scott looked sympathetically at Hannah and Samantha. Faye got up to get the box of tissues and brought them to Samantha, who looked up at her gratefully as she took one. Billy and Phoebe looked at each other with knowing eyes.

"I used to feel that way," said Faye. "I was just so hopeless all the time, as though there was no way out, and no way to stay in what I was doing either. It's a hard place to be."

"How does it feel to talk about this, Hannah?" asked Gale.

"It feels better for some reason," said Hannah. "I don't know why."

"How does it feel to cry, Samantha?" asked Gale.

"It feels scary," said Samantha. "I feel like a dolt. I'm really embarrassed," she said, sniffling.

"Who feels Samantha is a dolt?" asked Gale.

"I think she's a completely hopeless dolt," said Scott, smiling at Samantha.

Samantha giggled, mopping her eyes and blowing her nose. "What good is crying?" said Samantha. "It's a total waste of time. It's not as though anything gets accomplished by crying."

"Not true," said Gale. "Letting your feelings flow is important. But you seem to be very focused on accomplishing, Samantha. You know, one of the characteristics of people with eating problems is they always feel they have to be accomplishing something or producing or achieving or getting results. Who identifies with that?"

"I do," said Scott.

"I do, too," said Hannah. "If I'm not studying or eating, I have to be answering a letter or straightening a drawer. I just can't let myself be still."

"I vacuum my room sometimes six times a day. You should see my room. It looks like a lunatic lives there," admitted Samantha.

"I used to do that," said Faye. "Now I just sit down and wait until the urge to clean goes away."

"Ever since coming here," said Hannah, "I think I'm getting better. I mean, I'm talking more and everything. But I'm actually feeling worse."

"Me, too," said Samantha. She was relieved to hear Hannah talking about this. "It seems as though coming here and talking about myself is making me feel even worse and I hate it."

"When things are getting better, people often do feel

worse at first. That's because you're listening more carefully to your inner life," Gale explained.

"Oh, wonderful," remarked Phoebe. "You mean the better we get, the worse we're gonna feel?"

Scott laughed. "Yeah, what's the story here?"

Phoebe saw Daryl as she was coming out of the market. She had bought some brown rice and some chickpeas. She was going to help her mother make them for dinner with the fillet of sole. She'd also gotten some blueberries and strawberries.

Daryl was getting into his old, powder-blue Mustang convertible. When he saw Phoebe, he said, "Hey, Phoeb, what's cooking?"

Phoebe never knew how to answer Daryl when he talked to her. He always called her "Phoeb," and she liked that. She felt self-conscious and tongue-tied around him, though.

"Nothing much," answered Phoebe, sounding silly to herself.

"You're looking good," said Daryl. He smiled that smile

that melted Phoebe, and gave her the thumbs-up sign as he drove away.

Phoebe was rattled. Daryl had never said anything to her about how she looked. She naturally assumed that everybody did notice her appearance because she took up more space than everybody else did, but most people were tactful enough not to mention it.

When she arrived home, her mother was cutting up an onion. "Hi," said her mother. "How was your day?"

"Good," said Phoebe. "We did a print ad for Clairol. The hairdresser said I had pretty hair. It made me happy because hair can never get fat, so I was feeling pretty good until just now, when I bumped into Daryl."

She took the groceries out of the bag and put them on the counter. She looked pretty in a red T-shirt with black leggings and clogs. Little spots of pink had formed high on her cheeks.

"What happened with Daryl?" asked her mother, as she put the onion slices into a pan. "Is everything okay with his mother?" She looked a bit concerned.

Most of the neighborhood knew that Daryl's mother wasn't well. She was extremely overweight and had recently suffered a serious heart attack.

"I guess so," said Phoebe. "He seemed happy and everything. It's just that he told me I was looking good." She frowned. She sat at the kitchen table dejectedly.

"That's a disaster?" replied her mother playfully as she put the pan full of onions onto the stove.

"I don't know," sighed Phoebe. "I feel as though I've lost my privacy or something. I can't explain it, really."

The image of Daryl driving away, smiling at her, unsettled her and she couldn't understand why.

"Well," said her mother, "it usually feels good to have someone tell you that you look good."

Phoebe went up to her room to organize her closet and get it ready for the school season. Her pants were loose-fitting now. Her T-shirts were baggier and they looked much better than when they had pulled tightly across her ample chest. She was happy about the way she was looking in her clothes, but an underlying anxiety pulled at her.

After she'd finished reorganizing the clothes, she went down to get the *TV Guide*. As she was headed for the stairs again, she found herself walking into the kitchen. Her mother had dinner ready and had gone to take a shower.

She went to the cookie jar and, taking it off the shelf above the kitchen table, helped herself to a handful of rich, Danish butter cookies and poured herself a glass of milk. The house was quiet. Phoebe felt a delicious excitement. She ate four cookies before she had finished half the glass of milk. Her pulse began to race. She took another four cookies out of the jar and ate them dreamily. She stared at the cookie jar in the shape of a giant cupcake and thought it looked good enough to eat. When she looked into the jar for some more cookies, she noticed that there were only five left, so she went to the pantry, opened another of the tins and emptied eight of them into the jar. Then she ate the cookies remaining in the tin. Their sweetness washed over her in waves that transported her to an oblivion where the past and the future did not exist.

In all, she had eaten twenty-two cookies and drunk a quart of milk before dinner.

* * *

Samantha put on a pair of small pearl earrings, completing her outfit, then she vacuumed her room and waited for Len to pick her up. She had vacuumed her room only one other time that day. It was the first time in a long time she'd vacuumed less than three times in a single day. She had accomplished this amazing feat by forcing herself to do something else each time she had an impulse to clean. One time, she had put on an Alanis Morissette CD and made herself stay on her bed, listening until the whole thing was over. Once, she even went downstairs and ate half an apple.

She turned off the vacuum cleaner and put it away under the bed. Then she put on her Tori Amos CD, the one Lacey had given her for her last birthday. She checked herself in the mirror. Her ribs showed beneath her tight tank top with the little green satin bow, and her jeans were as baggy as ever. She'd been afraid that just going to Gale's would make her fat, but so far there had been no evidence of this at all.

Len said they didn't have to go to dinner if it made her uncomfortable, but she'd decided to try it, so they were going to the restaurant with the big salad bar that Samantha had suggested. She was excited about seeing Len, but she was nervous, too. What if he asked about one of her scars?

Her father didn't like her having boyfriends. He acted as though he owned her. When she was seeing Brian, she'd arrange to meet him somewhere other than at her house because her father would get such an attitude. Tonight, her father was at a town board meeting.

When Len and Samantha were leaving, her mother told them to be home by 1:00. Samantha was surprised that her mother hadn't asked her to be home earlier. What had happened to her mother? Samantha wondered about this as Len ushered her out the door and down the driveway to his old, gray Volvo.

Feeling tense, Samantha sat looking at her lap as Len drove through town to the Green Parrot restaurant. Len made conversation about his summer job at a landscaping company and about going away to college in January. His arms looked tan and strong from lifting and planting large trees all summer. Samantha liked how determined and independent Len seemed, that he was so practical yet such a lot of fun. He did the silliest imitations of people they knew and had a wonderful laugh that made her laugh, too.

When they arrived at the restaurant, Samantha was pleased to notice that the salad bar was well-stocked with vegetables, greens and beans. When she'd come back from the salad bar with her plate, Len looked at the lettuce and the leaves of spinach and the three red beans and the single slice of tomato, but he didn't say anything. He ordered a hamburger for himself and Diet Cokes for both of them. Samantha put some pepper on her salad, but didn't take any of the oil out of the cruet that sat on the table between them.

Len looked at her cutting the lettuce with a knife and fork. "You certainly are a dainty eater," he observed.

Samantha, feeling self-conscious, changed the subject to the colleges to which she was interested in applying.

By the time she had finished her greens, Len was ready to have a piece of pie. "I know you won't want dessert," he said as he ordered his pie.

"How do you know?" asked Samantha.

"Well," said Len, "it's obvious that you have anorexia."

Samantha was horrified. How had he realized? "How is it obvious?" she said.

"Well, you're so thin," he said, "and you've eaten only lettuce and three beans." He hesitated, seeing her stricken look. "I don't mind," he added.

But Samantha minded. She minded his knowing. She felt so ashamed, so exposed. She minded him having said that word, the one that showed that he'd seen her. He was diagnosing her! It felt as though he was pushing her away when he said that, pointing his finger at her.

"You look angry," he said, dismayed. "I was just trying to let you know I understand."

I just don't know what happened," cried Phoebe in group. "I just couldn't stop. It was like I was in a posthypnotic trance or something and my instruction had been 'eat the cookies, eat the cookies.' It wasn't as if I ate three or six either. I ate hundreds."

"Oh, I'll bet it wasn't hundreds," argued Faye.

"Well, I think I ate about two dozen," said Phoebe, deliberating. "Really, I did, and I drank a quart of milk, too. Before dinner! I'm truly hopeless!"

"What happened that day, Phoebe?" asked Gale. "Did anything unusual happen?"

"I don't think so," said Phoebe sadly.

"Think," prodded Gale.

"Well," said Phoebe, "I saw this boy I know, Daryl, and he told me I looked good. But why should that make me eat? It should have made me feel good. I think I'm crazy and hopeless."

"Yep, 'ol' crazy and hopeless Phoebe' is what we always call her," said Billy.

Phoebe started to laugh. She knew in her mind that she wasn't crazy and hopeless, but right now she was convinced she was.

"Well," said Faye, "you may feel crazy and hopeless, but that doesn't mean you are. Feelings aren't facts. Sometimes I believe I'm a blue fire engine, but that doesn't mean I am one."

"You believe you're a blue fire engine?" asked Scott.

"Oh, you know what I mean," said Faye. "But really, Phoeb, sometimes when someone tells me I look good I just want to punch 'em."

"But why?" asked Phoebe, puzzled.

"Because they're paying attention to what's on the outside."

"When Daryl told me I looked good," said Phoebe, "I felt I would have to start exercising more and eat even less and look even better, and then Daryl might ask me for a date, and then I would really faint, just from the anxiety of it all."

"I know what she means," said Faye. "She isn't ready for all this social development stuff or whatever. She's never even had a date, and the most popular boy in the whole school is telling her she looks good."

"I don't even believe him when he says that," said Phoebe. "Anyway, I guess I want to go back to the old, safe way."

"What's so good about the old, safe way?" asked Gale.

"Good?" said Phoebe incredulously. "About the old way? What could possibly be good about it? My father ridiculed me, and my thighs rubbed together, and I felt like a big blob. Nothing was good about the old way—nothing!"

"What was the old way doing for you?" persisted Gale.

"Well," said Phoebe thoughtfully, "I guess . . . I don't know. I guess it protected me from having to . . . I don't know . . . participate. It protected me from feeling I had to join the world."

Everyone was quiet, and Phoebe knew she had hit on something true. Being fat was safe. It was predictable, and the safety of it tasted almost as sweet as all the chocolate.

"I know how you feel," said Samantha. "The other night, Len told me he realized I was anorexic. I felt furious, and I couldn't understand why I felt that way because he said he didn't mind, but I felt like a lab specimen or something."

"Actually, though, he had come closer to you," said Scott softly.

"I guess that scares me," reflected Samantha.

❋ ❋ ❋

Samantha and Len were going to a party on Labor Day weekend. It was going to be a barbecue at the home of Len's brother. Samantha had met Len's parents, but not his brother and sister-in-law, and she was nervous. Meeting new people was always a problem for her and, when the contact had to do with food, it was especially hard. She thought of all the ways she could appear to have eaten without actually eating anything. She could go to the bathroom when the hamburgers were being served and linger there and then, when she came back, she would quietly pick up someone's empty plate, smeared with ketchup and grease and onions, and, when she was offered another hamburger, she could say, "Oh, no thanks, I'm stuffed."

When she got to the party, though, she saw at once that

this would never work. Len's family was small. His mother, father, brother and sister-in-law were the only ones at the party. After the burgers and franks had been cooked on the grill, Len's brother brought them inside. It was a drizzly afternoon, and the family gathered at the dining room table to eat. There was no way Samantha could pretend to have eaten.

When she sat down with her burger, smiling politely, she realized at once that she had to eat and look normal about it. She ate half the hamburger, and then, seeing that everyone else had finished every morsel on their plates and wanting to teach Len a lesson about having diagnosed her, she picked up the half-eaten burger, now cold with fat congealing around its edges, which disgusted her, and took one last bite. She hadn't eaten this much at one time in longer than she could remember.

Len's family joked about how much Len liked to eat. Len, who was tall and thin, had eaten two burgers and two franks and was now drinking a tall glass of root beer.

He looked approvingly at Samantha and said, "Yeah, I'm a pig, not like Sam here, who's so delicate."

He beamed at her, and she felt like a fat pig. *Delicate? I've eaten like a horse,* she thought, *and I'm a complete blob, a whale.*

Len kissed her for a long time when he took her home,

but she couldn't pay attention to what they were doing. She was too busy feeling blobbed out. They stood in the foyer in the dim light of the porch and held each other. Samantha had never felt this way about a boy before. Her jeans felt excruciatingly tight. She tried to smile up at Len when he left, but all she could think about was getting out of the jeans.

When she had taken them off, she looked at herself in the mirror and realized that she had lost her waistline. Her belly button was stretched out of shape by the bloat in her abdomen. She'd had several Diet Cokes that night out of nervousness and because she didn't want to talk too much. She would never let herself do this again. She felt she had to do something definite, something dramatic, to make her remember never to do this again, ever. The tension was building. Her body was an inflating balloon, unbearably distended, bursting with self-loathing, with pain, with disgust at herself, with anger at Len, with unrealized possibilities, with the fear of change, with the fear that nothing would change. She was so swollen that she could hardly feel herself. She had to make the pressure go away. She knew what to do. It was so simple.

She got out her cuticle scissors with the dainty, curving tips and sat on the bed. She told herself, *I need to see this scar every day to remind me how disgusting I was tonight.* She grasped the scissors and pierced the flesh on the back of her hand. Blood sprang out at once and spread quickly, making it hard for her to see the cut. She mopped at it with a tissue, then quickly made three other punctures, equidistant from one another. The wounds formed a circle of four dots in blood, which were now spreading into one another.

She sighed. She felt great relief. She had paid for her sin and had at the same time issued herself a warning. *You better be good now,* Samantha warned herself, *otherwise next time it will be worse.*

* * *

Daryl noticed Phoebe at the record shop looking at CDs of Nine Inch Nails and Van Morrison.

"You into that old Van Morrison stuff?" he said when she looked up at him standing nearby. His eyes were so blue they didn't look real.

"Oh, yeah," she said, "I am. Sometimes my father plays it at the studio during a shoot. It's really good."

"I'm into Van Morrison, too," said Daryl. "Say, you're

looking really good lately. What have you been up to? Going to the gym?"

Here he goes again, thought Phoebe. "Well, not the gym," said Phoebe shyly, "but I do exercise." She didn't want to launch into a discussion with him about low-fat eating. That would be so lame.

"Well, you're doing something right," Daryl said.

Oh, no, thought Phoebe, *I can't stand this. He's going to force me to say something dorky. Anyway, how can he say I'm looking great when I'm still so big?*

"Listen," said Daryl, "do you want to have some coffee?"

Oh, my God, thought Phoebe. "Sure," she said, making her voice sound even and natural while she jumped out of her skin.

They went next door to the big bookstore that had a café in it with fancy coffees and pretty pastries. Phoebe's mouth was dry with anxiety and dread.

"I'll have a decaf, please," said Phoebe. *Well,* she thought, *so far, so good. I got that right.*

Daryl ordered a hazelnut latté with a piece of gooey, chocolate-mousse cake.

When they sat down, Daryl said, "Would you tell me what you did to change? Could we talk about it? Do you mind?"

She minded completely, but those blue eyes implored.

"Why do you want to talk about it?" asked Phoebe, feeling suspicious.

"Well," Daryl began, "I'm seeing a girl now from another town. She needs help, and I want to let her know how to get it, you know, what help there is specifically. I saw you go into the guidance office a few times, and I figured it wasn't about colleges. What help would you need with that?"

Phoebe's reputation as a scholar was well known. *Now,* she thought, *he's spying on me.*

"I don't really know how I can help," said Phoebe, confused.

"Well, what made you go for help?" Daryl asked, sipping his latté.

"Isn't it obvious?" said Phoebe.

"Not really," said Daryl, "although if you mean your weight, I guess so."

"Everyone was always so cruel to me in school, even my own family," said Phoebe, suddenly inexplicably wanting to tell him everything. "And my friends, even them, they would whine about how awful it was to be fat, and it was torture." She sipped her coffee. She couldn't believe she was sitting there with him.

Daryl cut off a hunk of his cake and left it on his plate. Phoebe noticed the thick texture where it had stuck to the fork. She didn't crave it.

"Is that your girlfriend's problem? Her weight?" asked Phoebe.

"Yes," said Daryl, "she thinks she's fat. She's fine, really."

"Well, is she or isn't she?" asked Phoebe, intensely curious to know this vital fact.

"Want to see for yourself?" asked Daryl, eagerly reaching for his wallet in his back pocket.

"Yes," said Phoebe, "of course."

Daryl extracted a snapshot from his wallet and handed it across the table.

Phoebe saw a smiling, dark-haired girl at the beach. She was adorable, with jaw-length, shining hair and bangs cut straight across. She had a pixie face with a curving, bow-shaped upper lip. She was wearing a bright-pink one-piece bathing suit, and she was dancing with an inflatable mermaid—and she was chubby! Phoebe couldn't believe that the most popular boy in school, the handsomest and most accomplished boy, the boy over whom all the girls in all the grades swooned, was dating a chubby girl. She was almost the same size as Phoebe was now.

"She's pretty," said Phoebe, handing back the picture. "She's really pretty."

"Well, she thinks she isn't," said Daryl, "and it's really starting to get to me. I mean, I tell her how she looks great, and she spends half the night talking about how fat she is.

The other half of the time we have something great going. But this other thing, it's starting to wear me down. It's really boring, if you want to know the truth. Prettiness is only important in the first five minutes anyway. How someone makes you feel is more important. Girls just don't understand that," he said sadly.

He's brilliant. I love him, thought Phoebe.

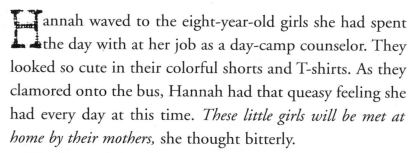

Hannah waved to the eight-year-old girls she had spent the day with at her job as a day-camp counselor. They looked so cute in their colorful shorts and T-shirts. As they clamored onto the bus, Hannah had that queasy feeling she had every day at this time. *These little girls will be met at home by their mothers,* she thought bitterly.

The heat of the day, penetrating and moist, enveloped her. She still had two hours before Kaneesha and Tanya would be finished working and they could meet.

She decided to browse the library for Wally Lamb's new book. It was only a two-mile walk, and then she would be a half mile from her house, which was not air-conditioned.

The Leeswood Free Library had an imposing brick façade, but the cool, quiet atmosphere was a relief from the brightness and heat of the street.

Even as a child, Hannah had always enjoyed coming to the library. She'd bring home videotapes that she and her mother could watch together. Her mother loved Audrey Hepburn and James Stewart and movies about animals. They must have watched *It's a Wonderful Life* and *Breakfast at Tiffany's* and *Bringing Up Baby* fifteen times. Thinking of the safety of those hours in her mother's bedroom made Hannah shudder as she walked through the reading room. A familiar head turned to glance up at Hannah as she walked toward the fiction section.

"Hi, Hannah," whispered Arlette as Hannah approached.

"Hey," said Hannah when she recognized the pert red mouth, the upturned nose.

Hannah's heart lurched. She hoped her discomfort didn't show. Hannah noticed Arlette's bare legs, smooth and tan, and her long elegant feet in their Birkenstocks. It was cool in the library, but Hannah could feel the beads of perspiration forming on her forehead and upper lip. She looked at her watch in order to have somewhere to place her gaze.

They chatted for a minute, then Arlette walked toward the checkout desk. Hannah noticed the way Arlette's hair shimmered as she walked away.

Adrianne Blaine glanced at her watch and tapped her foot impatiently as she gazed out the window. She was standing in the living room, which seemed smaller without the furniture that had given it meaning. The sofa on which Jessica and Matthew had spent countless hours watching TV was gone, but the rust-colored carpet that Matt would sit on with his Legos and his marble collection was still in place.

Adrianne could see the clear imprint of four little squares where the legs of the tweed chair in which Skye liked to read his books about the Civil War had been. Sometimes she felt as though their fourteen-year marriage had been a civil war.

Her relationship with Keith felt good. They both liked to drink a few beers, go dancing, and gamble in Atlantic City. Skye was so serious all the time. Keith managed a rock band from Atlanta. That's where they were moving. She would swing by Matthew's day camp in a cab, pick him up, and go directly to the airport. Matt didn't like Keith or the idea of moving, but he liked rock bands, and Keith had promised him a guitar when they moved.

She saw the cab pull up and sighed. The sigh was like a period at the end of this part of her life.

* * *

Phoebe, having made certain that the studio was locked up and that the alarm had been properly set, began her walk across Manhattan to Pennsylvania Station for the hour-long train ride that would take her home. Her father and the rest of the staff had spent the day on location in Connecticut, shooting stills in various gardens for a new perfume campaign. Phoebe had fielded phone calls and accepted deliveries, and had lots of time to herself in between. She'd brought Ali MacGraw's yoga video with her to work. She'd sat on the floor of the enormous, sky-lit main room of the studio following Ali MacGraw's instructions. The yoga made her feel calm and strong.

At 5:00, though, she felt jumpy. She was going to meet Daryl. Daryl's mother and Phoebe's father shared the same birthday: August 29. Phoebe had arranged a surprise party for her father at his studio and had ordered a cake in the shape of a huge roll of Kodak film, but she was also going to get him a book about American art. Daryl wanted to get his mother a big book with pictures of quilts. Quilts were his mother's passion, and she spent all her spare time creating them. Phoebe and Daryl were meeting at the bookstore to buy their parents' birthday gifts.

Phoebe and Daryl had gotten close. Though Phoebe missed Jessica painfully, she felt even closer to Daryl in ways that she never had with Jessica. Jessica hated plump bodies; Daryl loved a girl who had one. The only topic Phoebe couldn't talk to Daryl about was how she felt about him. But he was sensitive. He knew.

Hannah, Kaneesha, Tanya, Doug and someone named Lyle, whom Hannah had never met, had been to The Speakeasy, a local café, for dinner, and then to a concert by two bands, Angry Salad and her favorite, Dracula Jones. Doug had dropped Hannah off and would be picking her up the next day to go to the beach where volleyball would be the main focus. Hannah kicked off her black platform sneakers and sat on her bed, her body still resonating with the vibrations of the music. There was no way she could sleep.

Hannah's grandmother, whom she had visited earlier that afternoon, had given her a big box of photographs, and she decided to look at them now. There were some photos of her as a baby with her mother. She hadn't seen those in a long time. In the pictures, her mother was very thin. In pictures of her mother taken before she had given birth to Hannah, she wasn't thin at all. Hannah turned the pictures over to make sure of the dates. Then she wondered if her own birth hadn't been what had made her mother stop eating properly. Although Gale had encouraged her not to dwell on nonproductive lines of thinking such as this, once the speculation took hold it grew roots.

She'd had no intention of bingeing. She'd had a great time with her friends, and the music was fantastic. As soon as she started on the ham sandwich, though, it was as though another person had invaded her, a person she didn't want anywhere near her, the one who ate like a monster. She vomited up all the food, and then, exhausted, she needed to rest. All she needed was a good night's sleep. Then she could think about all of this in the morning and talk about it in group on Tuesday night.

She went into her bathroom, intending to take two aspirin. As she swallowed them, she noticed her face in the medicine-cabinet mirror. Her skin was blotchy, and her face looked puffy and distorted. As she looked deeply into her own eyes, she imagined she saw an old woman there, her grandmother. She wanted to sleep for a long time. She needed to sleep and to avoid thinking that, no matter how great the music was, no matter how good things got, her mother was still dead.

She opened the aspirin bottle and swallowed ten aspirin. Her body ached. She needed something for her muscle pain. She saw the Advil, opened the bottle and took ten. Her red eyes looked back at her as she closed the cabinet. Her head felt unbearably stuffy at this time of year. She opened the cabinet again and took the box of Benadryl, swallowing six. Then she felt satisfied that she could sleep.

Daryl Morgenstern felt unsettled as he locked the clinic's back door and walked to his car. He loved working at the animal hospital each summer, but he felt anxious about his mother.

She hadn't been well since her doctor had changed her heart medication. The cardiologist always said the same thing to her: She needed desperately to lose weight and exercise was essential. His mother had struggled to take off weight for years. She'd been more than twice as large as most other women for as long as Daryl could remember. He was proud of her work as a counselor at Planned Parenthood. While Daryl had been embarrassed by her size when he was younger, he'd gotten over that.

It was after his father had died last summer that his mother's health had deteriorated. She'd had her first heart attack exactly one year to the day after his father's death. Daryl worried about what would become of his younger twin sisters if anything happened to his mother. That was how he phrased his fear: He would think "if anything happened" rather than "if she were to die." He knew that money for the girls was there. His father had seen to that, and he would be off to Tufts in another two weeks, but where would the children go? Who would raise them? Anger towards his mother rose up in him suddenly. How could she trade bags of potato chips for taking care of her family?

Anxiously, he drove home, picturing her dead, a huge mound of quilts on her bed. He heard music coming from the twins' bedroom as he came into the house. Monica was their favorite this week.

When the group assembled, Hannah wasn't there.

"Has anyone heard from Hannah?" asked Gale.

No one had.

"Let me call her," said Gale. She walked to her desk, looked in her Rolodex for Hannah's number, then dialed quickly. After asking for Hannah and listening for a minute, she said, "Hospital?" Then she hesitated again, listening. "Oh, I see. Well, thank you very much."

The group was wide-eyed at the word *hospital*.

"Hannah swallowed a couple of dozen pills last night," said Gale, "aspirin and Advil and Benadryl. Her father said she was at home now, but asleep." She sighed. "So, how do you all feel about this?"

"I feel awful," cried Phoebe. "I was talking to her practically every day. She never told me she had something like this up her sleeve." Phoebe began to weep suddenly. "I feel so betrayed!"

"I knew she was feeling uncomfortable about keeping her food, but I didn't ever think she'd try to kill herself," said Samantha.

"Well, we don't know about that yet," cautioned Gale.

"When can we talk to her?" asked Phoebe. "I feel a little afraid of her now."

"So do I," said Samantha. "I feel as though she told us all to go to hell."

"I feel that way, too," agreed Scott.

"I have something I need to tell the group," said

Samantha softly. She hadn't intended to talk about this, about the cutting.

"What is it?" asked Gale.

"I know that what Hannah did was very terrible and important and that she had to go to the hospital and everything, and I don't want to take up all the group's time, but I need to tell you that I cut myself again."

"What happened?" asked Scott.

"Well," answered Samantha, "remember I told you about going to Len's barbecue? I ate there. I had to. Everyone was sitting around the table, and I felt so full and so like a whale that I had to remind myself never to do that again, so I cut myself to remind myself."

Phoebe said, "Sam, what are you doing to yourself?"

Samantha began to cry. "I don't say to you, 'Phoebe, what are you doing to yourself?' when you eat two dozen cookies. I never say that."

Phoebe was horrified.

"That was brave," said Gale to Samantha. "You were angry. You said how you felt. How did it feel to hear that, Phoebe?"

"It felt . . . it felt awful!" Phoebe slumped in her chair. "I feel sick over it. I'm getting nauseous because I see that Sam is so right. My stuffing is as disgusting to her as her cutting herself is to me. I never thought of it that way, believe it or not."

She turned to Sam. "I'm sorry, Sam. I was just being

caring . . . or thought I was," said Phoebe dejectedly.

"I know," said Samantha. "I didn't mean to blurt that out."

"I know."

"Did you tell Len about it?" asked Faye.

"No, of course not. I wasn't even going to tell you guys. I don't want him to think I'm a freak."

"Well," said Gale, "you once said you wished that someday you could have a truly close relationship."

"So?" said Samantha.

"So, why don't you pick someone to be Len and tell him? Tell him as though nothing he knew about you could possibly turn him off."

Samantha looked around the room. The group waited expectantly.

"I don't want to do this."

Everyone was quiet. The soft sounds of traffic blended with the sound of crickets.

Samantha sighed. She crossed her legs, then recrossed them in the other direction.

Faye coughed.

"You don't have to do it if you don't want to," said Gale.

"I pick Scott to be Len," said Samantha suddenly to Scott who was sitting beside her.

"Okay," said Gale, "good. So, where would you tell Len about this?"

"In the car, I guess," decided Samantha, "because he wouldn't be looking at me if he was driving."

"Okay," said Gale. "Go."

Samantha took a deep breath. She bit her lower lip. She squeezed her eyes shut tightly for a second and then opened them again. She began, "There's something about myself I'm really afraid to tell you about, Len."

Len (Scott) reached over and placed his hand over Samantha's without taking his eyes off the imaginary road. "What is it, Sam?" he asked. He turned the wheel as though he was making a right turn.

"I'm afraid you'll think I'm nuts, a mental case," said Samantha.

"Well," said Len (Scott), "I already think you're mental."

The group laughed. He had said this quietly, placatingly, as though he were talking to a mental patient who might become violent at any moment.

Samantha laughed, too. She felt loosened up now and had no trouble continuing. She placed her hand over Len's and squeezed it. "What it is, is that sometimes I cut myself."

"You cut yourself?" asked Len (Scott). "On purpose?"

"See?" said Samantha, pulling her hand away. She crossed her arms in front of her chest. "I knew you would think I was crazy."

Len (Scott) pulled the imaginary car over to the side of

the imaginary road and pulled up the imaginary emergency brake.

Scott was displaying quite a talent for mime. The group was enraptured.

He faced Samantha, gently taking her hands in his own and looking into her eyes. "I find you very lovely, Samantha," he said, "and very sane. If you are doing something crazy-sounding to yourself, I'm sure there is a good reason for it. Now, tell me, where are these cuts?"

"Well," replied Samantha, "there's one right here." She pulled her sleeve up to her elbow, revealing a soft, downy arm across which were several horizontal scars. "I do this with cuticle scissors or tweezers. I did one the other night after the barbecue, in fact."

He pulled her to him and held her.

Samantha began to cry. "You're unrealistically wonderful," she sobbed into Scott's chest. "I can't imagine Len being this wonderful." She looked up and smiled at him.

"How did it feel to imagine telling Len that stuff, Samantha?" asked Gale.

"I would never actually tell Len," Samantha assured her, "but it felt wonderful to tell Scott." Samantha smiled at him again.

"How did it feel to have Samantha tell you such personal things, Scott?" asked Gale.

"It felt wonderful," answered Scott. "It felt as though she really trusted me and really knew I cared about her. It almost felt as though she was telling me she loved me."

Hannah sat up in bed, feeling groggy and ashamed. Her peach bedspread strewn with daisies was bunched up at the foot of the bed. It looked carefree and spent, like the end of a busy, sunny, summer day. Hannah hated sunny days. They reminded her even more of her own gloom.

She was talking on the phone with Gale, who was telling her not to be so hard on herself.

"Even my own father doesn't know anything about me," wailed Hannah. "I'm never going to be able to tell him, either. I can't ever tell him that I'm a bulimic lesbian and that what I need is a complete makeover, a total personality transplant. It would drive him nuts! It's driving me nuts! And after what he went through with my mother!" She started to cry.

"I'm totally ashamed and fed up," added Hannah. "I never meant to kill myself, though. I just wanted to make sure I could sleep. I did want out, but only out of my head, not my life. Maybe that's what my mother thought she was doing, starving to take her mind off her mind or something. Oh, God, I'm so confused."

"Actually, you're getting clearer by the minute, Hannah," said Gale softly. "Maybe that's what's so confusing."

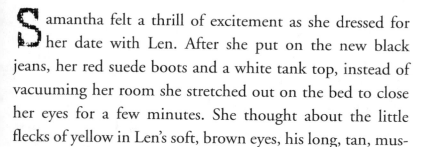

Samantha felt a thrill of excitement as she dressed for her date with Len. After she put on the new black jeans, her red suede boots and a white tank top, instead of vacuuming her room she stretched out on the bed to close her eyes for a few minutes. She thought about the little flecks of yellow in Len's soft, brown eyes, his long, tan, muscular arms, the gentle way he looked at her.

When she got into his car, she found herself saying, "I need to talk to you about something."

He leaned to kiss her on the cheek, but, instead of having his eyes closed as usual, he looked at her suspiciously.

"What's up, Sam? You look great, by the way."

She heard the anxious tone in his voice. It was too late to back out now. She had begun.

"I wouldn't tell this to just anyone," she began. She hesitated.

He hadn't started the car yet. He had his fingers on the ignition key. Now he dropped his hand into his lap and then quickly put his arm around her.

"What is it, Sam?" he asked, now with his arms around her, and with that tone of concern in his gentle voice.

She relaxed a bit. The air was the perfect temperature. It felt silky on Samantha's face. She felt an intense peace.

"I sometimes cut myself when I feel bad," she announced simply.

"You cut yourself?" he said, sounding puzzled.

"Yes, I cut myself. Here, look." She showed him, holding up the back of her left hand for him to inspect.

He slid closer to her, brought her hand closer to his face and kissed it. He closed his eyes as he did this and then opened them and said, "I've read about things like this, but I didn't know if you . . ."

He held her hands in both of his and said sternly, "See here," with mock solemnity, "there is no need for you to do that to yourself anymore."

"I know," she said softly. "I know there isn't."

Samantha felt a pleasant warmth spreading through her body.

Len squeezed her hand. "Do you want to talk more or do you want to go and talk on the way?"

"We can drive, if you want to," she replied. She didn't know what she wanted to do. Another car drove toward them down the street, headlights glaring.

"It felt so good to tell you this," said Samantha.

At first, Daryl felt relieved to hear music coming from the twins' room on the second floor of the house. At least they were at home. His mother hadn't been alone. Then he felt outraged that the music was so loud. How could she rest?

Since her heart attack, his mother had moved into the spare room off the kitchen. Climbing to the second floor was too dangerous, especially with the additional strain of her excess weight.

With the sound of Monica accompanying him, Daryl entered the house by the side door at the end of the drive-way where the hydrangea was in full bloom, the fat, round, blue blossoms forming a polka-dot pattern against the dark, green foliage. The music sounded a bit muffled as he walked through the kitchen, and he was comforted that it didn't sound as loud as it had when he'd heard it through the open window. There were dishes in the sink. *The twins will never learn,* he thought. *Don't they realize how ill Mom is?*

Her door was open. Daryl could see her lying on her back on her bed, the still-unfinished red, white and blue quilt folded neatly on the chair beside her.

"Mom?" he said. He let a few seconds pass. Now the sound of the Spice Girls vibrated rhythmically, a pumping heartbeat, as though the ceiling, the whole house was breathing hard.

His mother didn't answer. She wasn't moving.

His heart accelerated suddenly, startling him. He could hear his blood roaring through his head.

He raced around to the other side of the four-poster bed. He fumbled with the phone on the table, his fingers clumsy, huge, moving in slow motion as he dialed 911. He called out for the twins.

Then he called Phoebe. She was the one he wanted to talk to, the one he felt would best understand.

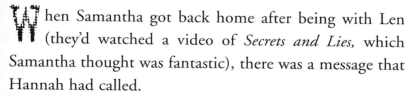

When Samantha got back home after being with Len (they'd watched a video of *Secrets and Lies,* which Samantha thought was fantastic), there was a message that Hannah had called.

"It doesn't matter how late you come in," the message said. "Please call me back."

It was 12:45 in the morning, but Samantha dialed Hannah, who answered right away.

"Sam," said Hannah, "I had to speak to you. Where have you been all day? Nobody is home anymore. Anyway, as soon as I woke up and realized I'd missed group, I felt awful. I thought you would all think I tried to kill myself or something."

"What happened?" asked Samantha, sitting on her bed and pulling off one of the red suede boots with some difficulty. She felt pleased that Hannah cared enough to call her.

"Well, I just wanted to make sure I could sleep. I needed a vacation from my head, an escape. Do you know what I mean?"

"Do I," said Samantha, pulling off the other boot. She thought of how it felt to cut herself. She wasn't trying to do away with herself, just with a certain state of mind. "I understand."

"I know," said Hannah.

"Were you out with Len when I called?"

"Yes. We hung out at his house, watched a video. It was cool. He's very understanding. I was even able to tell him that I cut myself."

"How were you ever, ever able to do that?" said Hannah, amazed.

"I don't know how I did it," said Samantha. "Rehearsing in group made me do it, I think. Anyway, are you feeling all right now? What did they do to you in the hospital?"

"Oh, they pumped my stomach and kept me there for a few hours, and then I was able to come home. My dad was really upset. He said I must be crazy. Do you think I'm crazy?"

"Well, look who you're asking," said Samantha, and both girls laughed.

❊ ❊ ❊

Marge Rosen looked out her living-room window and saw Samantha walking across the lawn from the driveway. It was two weeks into the fall term. The shrubs in front were surrounded by the first of the falling leaves, which blew across the lawn in swirls.

Samantha, wearing a short, green cotton skirt and a white T-shirt, still looked very thin, thought Marge. Some things had improved with Samantha, though. She was being more civil to her sister, Patty, for one thing.

"Oh, hi, Mom," said Samantha, startled to see her mother standing just inside the door.

Samantha headed for the stairs, but before she reached the first one, her mother said, "Sam, could we talk?"

"Uh . . . I guess so," answered Samantha, wondering what was going on now.

"I notice you haven't been vacuuming your room as much."

"Yeah, well, I've been seeing Len a lot and there's school and . . ."

"Samantha, I'm not complaining. I'm glad. It's not natural for a girl your age to spend so much time cleaning."

"Well," said Samantha, "I know I've been a little weird."

"You seem as though you're not as tense, Sam," observed Marge. "I'm glad."

"Me, too."

She felt awkward standing inside the front door talking to her mother, but it was better than talking to her from the opposite side of the bedroom door, like inmates in adjoining cells.

* * *

Gale Holland held a large mug of mint tea and looked out the kitchen window at her September garden, where snapdragons still bloomed beside chrysanthemums and a few late roses. It was Sunday, and she was keeping her promise to herself to pull out weeds.

She took the phone outside with her and placed it on a boulder while she worked. The earth smelled sweet, insects buzzed, birds sang, and she hardly noticed the phone ringing. Finally, she brushed the soil off her gloves, picked up the phone and said, "Hello. Gale Holland here, along with about fifty earthworms."

"Gale?" said Samantha tentatively.

"Yes. Is this Samantha?"

"Yes. You recognize my voice."

"Sure," said Gale, leaning backward to stretch. "What's up?"

"Could I talk to you for a few minutes? I know it's Sunday, but . . ."

"Sure," said Gale. "I'm glad you called, Samantha. You're not famous for being able to reach out."

"I know, but if every one of your clients called you every time they felt bad, you'd be a lunatic," said Samantha.

"Well, I already am a lunatic," said Gale calmly. "So, what's happening in your day?"

"Well, I've been thinking that I don't think I should continue in the group."

"And why is that?" asked Gale, getting ready for an explanation of clever and interesting dimensions.

"Well, I feel that everyone else in group is getting better, and I'm still eating bagel breakfasts and lettuce dinners. I feel bad when I compare myself."

Gale took off the gardening gloves, ran her fingers through her hair and sat down on the boulder. "Go on," she said.

"I don't think I'll ever change."

"You didn't think you'd ever tell Len about the cutting either, but since you've been in group, you told him, didn't you?" asked Gale.

"Yes," agreed Samantha, "but I don't think I'll ever get the food right."

"Oh," said Gale, "so you want to quit everything because one thing is out of place. Samantha, everything doesn't have to be completely perfect all the time. This is all-or-none thinking."

"But why go on if I'm not getting it?" persisted Samantha.

Gale said, "Just because you feel you are ruining your health and possibly your whole life with your undereating doesn't mean you can't enjoy yourself by learning better communication, which you are learning in group, Samantha. You are already punishing yourself with the undereating and the cutting. You don't have to punish yourself more *because* you're undereating. You don't have to punish yourself because you aren't 100-percent perfect at this exact minute. Enough with the punishment. Let it stop here."

Samantha got it. "Okay," she agreed, "I see what you're saying."

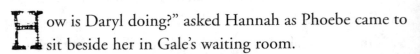

ow is Daryl doing?" asked Hannah as Phoebe came to sit beside her in Gale's waiting room.

It was a cool evening and both girls wore sweaters, Hannah's gray, Phoebe's dark green. They were the first to arrive for the group.

"Not so good," reported Phoebe, taking off her green backpack and setting it on the floor. "He still feels that if he had stayed home from work that day, if he hadn't gone to work . . ."

"But his mother was taking a nap," said Hannah. "Even

if he had been home that day, he wouldn't have gone into her bedroom every five minutes, would he?"

"Possibly," said Phoebe sadly.

"He wouldn't have been checking a million times to see if she was still breathing," insisted Hannah. "It's not his fault that she died."

"Well, he still feels it is."

"Well, I know how he feels," said Hannah.

Faye, Billy and Scott arrived all at once, followed closely by Samantha.

"How's Daryl doing?" asked Scott, just as Gale leaned around the corner and they followed her into the office. On Gale's desk was a huge pot of white chrysanthemums.

"I brought Daryl the exact same ones," said Phoebe.

Phoebe looked beautiful. She was still heavier than what she called "normal people," but she didn't want to worry about her weight anymore, even though her father clearly wanted her to. The bones in her face had begun to show. She had cut her hair so that the bouncy, brown curls fell to just above her shoulders.

"I think Daryl could really use some therapy," Phoebe said.

"I second that emotion," agreed Hannah.

This was Hannah's first group session since she had taken so many pills.

"How are you feeling, Han?" Billy asked her.

Hannah had received a call from everyone in the group. She felt that these people really cared, but she was eager to take the focus off herself.

"Oh, I'm fine now," she said. "How are you doing, Sam?"

Everyone knew of Samantha's anxieties about Len going away to college.

"I'm worried," said Samantha.

"Well," said Faye sympathetically, "just remember: Absence makes the heart grow fonder."

"And the girl grow lonelier," said Samantha plaintively. "Maybe absence even makes the heart go *wander*. His heart, anyway."

"Well, maybe you could let yourself enjoy him while he is here," offered Billy. "Maybe you could enjoy what's going on now while he is here, and start suffering later."

"I can't do that," said Samantha. "I have to rehearse the suffering. I have to be prepared."

Everyone laughed, including Samantha, but it didn't make her feel any better.

✳ ✳ ✳

Hannah sat in her advanced English class, feeling proud of herself. Mrs. Posner had singled out Hannah's Pro-Choice essay as exemplary and she had read it to the class. Hannah was proud also because she hadn't purged in eleven whole days. She had binged, but on wholesome foods like fruit. Although she hadn't actually gained weight, she felt like a total blob. Feeling as fat as she did, eleven days without a purge was a major feat.

Arlette was in the class, too. Hannah could see the curve of Arlette's neck where it disappeared into her gray angora sweater. Arlette had beautiful ears, Hannah noticed. Today she wore dangling pearl earrings in the shape of teardrops.

The class members were gathering up their books when Arlette suddenly appeared at Hannah's elbow.

"Hi," said Arlette. "What do you think of Posner so far?"

"She's great," said Hannah, "so far."

Among her books, Arlette was carrying one called *On Longing*. The title alone made Hannah want to know Arlette better.

"Want to have coffee or something?" Hannah asked.

Autumn was in full swing. Leaves blew around the village streets and pumpkins were appearing on porches and in shop windows.

Gale wrote her progress notes and thought about how lovely Phoebe was looking and how, even with occasional setbacks, she was continuing to lose weight. Her father had taken a beautiful photograph of her that she'd sent to Daryl.

Gale thought about Hannah and how, even though she was still purging, she did so with far less frequency. She was coming for individual sessions and was even planning on asking her father to come into some sessions with her.

Samantha was still not eating nearly enough, but she was eating a bit more. Also, she was not cleaning her room six times a day. She hadn't cut herself in over five weeks.

Gale expected some trouble though when Len left for Rhode Island. He was starting school in the January term, but he was going to look for an apartment and a job in Providence just after Thanksgiving.

In addition, Samantha's parents were having some problems. It looked as though they would be separating. Samantha, Patty and their mother would continue to live in the house, but their father would move to an apartment near the college where he taught. Samantha's mother, Marge, had gotten a job as a receptionist at a local drug and alcohol treatment center, and Samantha had offered to help her get more friendly with computers.

* * *

Molly and Michael McIntyre sat in their family room, looking out at the fall garden. Molly was happy. They were planning a surprise party for Phoebe's late-November birthday. They sat companionably in their sweatshirts and jeans, discussing Phoebe.

"We can invite everyone in her group," said Molly.

"And all those skinny friends of hers," added Michael.

"How about Daryl?" she asked with a puzzled expression. "I don't know if he's coming home for Thanksgiving." She made some notes on her legal pad.

"Invite him anyway," said Michael, "just in case."

"He has a girlfriend," remarked Molly, putting down her pen.

"Invite him anyway," said Michael.

Molly picked up her pen again. "Phoebe's crazy about him." Molly added Daryl's name to the guest list. "Should we invite his girlfriend, too?"

"Yes," replied Michael, without hesitation.

"But won't that be awkward for Phoebe?" said Molly, with concern.

"Maybe, but he's not going to be seriously interested in Phoebe anyway until she drops a few more pounds."

"His girlfriend is chubby," Molly reminded him, "and anyway, how many pounds do you consider a few? Five?"

"At least thirty-five," replied Michael. He took a sip of his white wine as though to punctuate his remark.

"You think appearances are more important than anything else," said Molly accusingly.

Michael considered this, cocking his head. "Appearances and money are tied for importance."

"You're terrible," said Molly, half affectionately, half critically.

"Let's have a themed party for Phoebe," said her father. "The theme could be 'Phoebe in Wonderland' and I could have the prop man build some huge furniture so that sitting in it would make people feel tiny, like Alice when she ate that cookie that made her shrink. We could make it a tea party."

* * *

On October 28, the Tuesday group members became apprehensive.

"There's all that food around," Hannah said. "All that Halloween candy is coming. Everywhere you go, there's candy now. Even at the bank. Even at the dentist's office. It's bizarre."

"Food is like that horrible villain that won't die even after you shoot it over and over," said Billy, who loved horror movies. "I can't stand the idea of Thanksgiving. I know I'm going to have that huge meal that leaves me with a hangover."

"It's impossible *not* to eat that huge meal though," said Faye. "How can you sit down with your family and not eat?"

"How can you sit down with the family *and* eat?" mumbled Scott, more to himself than anyone else.

"One meal that makes you feel full isn't going to change anybody's weight substantially," said Gale. "It's all those sweet potatoes with marshmallows in them that we keep eating all the way until Christmas, all those insidious left-overs that get us, isn't it?"

"Yeah," agreed Billy, "the leftovers. Hah! I eat them until after New Year's."

"I would encourage all you guys to concentrate on the people at the table rather than on the food at the table," suggested Gale. "That way, you might even have a good time."

"Doubtful with my family," said Scott. "Heaven forbid, a good time."

"That's true," said Billy. "One meal doesn't make a significant difference. I've made a study of it." Billy was always making studies of things. He worked at a research firm and had access to all sorts of data and computer programs that could compare everything to everything else.

"I feel scared," admitted Samantha. "My grandparents and everyone are coming down from Binghamton, and we always have this huge, really fattening meal."

"What can you do to make the holidays bearable, gang?" asked Gale.

"I could call people," suggested Hannah.

"You could call me," said Scott. "I'm going to be home moping after dinner."

"We could have a phone mope together," said Hannah.

"Great," said Scott, "a phone mope. Just what I need for dessert."

"And could I call you, too, Faye?" asked Hannah shyly. Hannah was intimidated by Faye because Faye was so shy and awkward, but there was something about Faye that reminded Hannah of her mother, and she wanted to reach out to Faye.

"Definitely," said Faye.

Billy turned to Phoebe. "What if I call you, Phoebe?" he asked.

"That would be great," said Phoebe. "Daryl is taking his girlfriend to his aunt's in Pennsylvania to be with the twins."

Samantha said, "I'm going to have dinner with my mom and grandparents, and dessert with Len's family. Ugh. Dessert! My dad is going to see his family in Riverdale."

"What can you do to make yourself more comfortable with all this food stuff, Samantha?" asked Gale.

Samantha looked at the ceiling as images of drumsticks and pumpkin pie swam before her eyes. "Maybe I can just . . . I don't know . . . accept that food is something I'm going to be uncomfortable with. I can't be different than I am. That might help."

"Brilliant!" said Gale.

Hannah said, "I can tell myself I can always throw up if I absolutely must, but I can try to talk myself through it first. Then, if talking to myself doesn't work, I can always revert."

"And then what?" asked Gale.

"And then I'm not supposed to beat myself up when I do revert and throw up. But I'm still having trouble with that part."

* * *

When Phoebe got into her room, she locked the door, grabbed her phone and went into the bathroom with it. She dialed Gale's number.

When Gale answered, she said, "I'm so sorry to have called you on a Saturday, but I feel so ashamed. I binged on all the Halloween candy at my dad's studio this afternoon, and he caught me at it, eating a big handful of chicken feed, that disgusting candy the color of traffic cones. How can anyone eat that stuff? How can *I* eat it? How can they feed it to children? Why do I get like this?"

"What's going on with you, Phoebe?" asked Gale. "What were you thinking about today?"

"I think about Daryl, and I just don't know what to do with my feelings about him," wailed Phoebe. "I guess I take my mind off all that by putting my mind on how stuffed I feel. Then I can bypass the whole reality loop, huh?"

"Yep," said Gale, "it's that old reality loop. You can speed right past that exit."

"I know," said Phoebe. "Hannah said that when she binges now, it's not taking her mind off what she's trying to take it off of. She's scared."

"Are you scared, too?" asked Gale.

"Terrified," said Phoebe.

* * *

Hannah sat at home, deliberating whether to eat or not to eat. Her bedroom was cozy, and she wore her blue, terry-cloth robe and fuzzy orange slippers in the shape of carrots that her grandmother had given her the previous Christmas. Looking at them usually made her smile; not this time, though.

She heard her father open the front door of the house, put down his keys, rifle through the mail, and walk upstairs.

He was surprised to find the door to her room wide open, with Hannah sitting on her bed atop the daisy-patterned bedspread.

"Hi. What's up, hon?" her dad said nervously, looking at his watch. "What are you doing at home on a Saturday night?"

"I'm moping," replied Hannah, taking a big risk with this remark. Would he understand? Gale had encouraged each of the group members to concentrate for a few minutes a week on feeling whatever it was that was telling them to use food to avoid focusing on their feelings.

"Sounds gloomy," said her father. "Why aren't you out?"

She couldn't explain that she felt too fat to go out. Instead, she said, "I had a paper to write and I didn't feel like going out anyway. And I've been feeling sad today . . . about Mom."

She let this remark register. Another risk. They seldom discussed feelings, only facts, logistics, arrangements, who would be home for dinner and when.

"How can I help you?" he asked, coming and sitting on the bed. He felt awkward, huge in the girlish room. He noticed the sadness in her eyes. It frightened him.

He looks so big in here, she thought. *Big and comforting.*

"It might help if you'd come to therapy with me," she blurted.

He looked pained suddenly, as though struck. He hesitated. He'd expected something about clothes, allowances, her friends. He cleared his throat, buying time.

Finally, he said, "Is that really necessary, sweetheart?" He hadn't called her "sweetheart" since she was eight. "That kind of thing makes me nervous," he said.

He was raised to believe that there was nothing that good hard work couldn't fix. You didn't go running to other people, particularly total strangers, to whine and complain. A priest maybe, but even then only in the direst of circumstances. Otherwise, you fixed things yourself or you grinned and bore the pain. This therapy stuff, that was for the very weak or the very rich, who had nothing better to do with their time and money than analyze their own thoughts. It was all right for Hannah: She studied psychology and needed to know this sort of thing about herself.

Tony Bonanti felt as though he was looking at his daughter now from across a huge chasm, that if he moved toward her he might step off the edge and tumble into a dark and terrifying unknown.

Hannah wasn't surprised by his response, but she wished it could have been different.

* * *

Daryl wrote his e-mail address on the back of a yellow receipt from Eddie Bauer and handed it to Phoebe. They sat side by side at the edge of the wharf. The setting sun had turned the sky purple, the water pink and the huge moon bright orange. Phoebe loved this time of day and this time of year because it was associated in her mind with a new school term and unmarked notebooks, and brought new beginnings and a fresh start. A cool breeze brought the scent of the ocean, faraway places and possibilities. The air was so pure that they could see clear across Long Island Sound to Connecticut.

Daryl had started at Tufts and had come back home for the weekend. His twin sisters were in school in Lancaster, where the Pennsylvania branch of the family lived.

"They'll be all right," said Daryl, as though to reassure himself.

He was holding a bunch of keys on a chain. He looked down at them. A green medallion—the size of his palm and in the shape of a four-leaf clover, bearing the words "good luck"—hung from the chain. Phoebe had given it to him as a going-away present.

They could hear seagulls and the sounds of engines starting up as the car ferry from Bridgeport boarded its last few passengers.

"Thanks for the gift, Phoeb," said Daryl, raising his head to look at her.

Phoebe was smiling, but there were tears in her eyes.

✻ ✻ ✻

Len and Samantha sat in Len's car, parked in Len's drive-way. They weren't going or coming from anywhere. They were in there for the privacy. Samantha wore her new, black leather jacket, a white silk scarf, and her softest jeans. Len wore a sad expression above his black turtleneck.

"What are we going to do about dating other people?" asked Samantha anxiously, shyly.

This was a topic that so terrified both of them that they hadn't had the courage to approach it before. He was leaving in less than an hour.

"Do you want to date other people?" she asked, her voice tense.

"Do you?" he replied.

This was not the response she would have preferred.

"No," she said. "I just want to concentrate on you," she added bravely.

"Me, too," said Len.

"You just want me to concentrate on you, too?" said Samantha.

They both laughed.

"I won't date anyone else, either," said Len, "and we can just keep asking each other about this each time I come home for the holidays and stuff. That will give us the chance to change our minds if we need to."

Samantha's mouth felt dry and tasted like pennies.

"I'm going to feel as though I'm waiting for the executioner when holidays come around," reflected Samantha.

"Well, what about me?" said Len. "I could come home, and you could axe me."

Yeah, right, thought Samantha, *like* I'm *going to date someone else; like* I'm *going to go through the agony of letting someone else know me. No way.*

"Your parents are standing at the front door, pointing at their watches," observed Samantha angrily. "You'd better go."

"D ad?" called Samantha as she let herself into her father's new apartment. She had the keys to two houses now. This was her first visit to her father's new home.

Nat Rosen came out of the bedroom to greet her. They perched uneasily, facing each other, on the edges of their armchairs, Samantha's dusty pink, Nat's turquoise. This had been a model apartment. It was brand-new and slickly furnished.

Nat observed that Samantha had not gained any weight, but that she was looking prettier, and was less stiff in the way she sat and moved.

Samantha noticed that her father looked older and grayer, especially surrounded by everything so new and modern. The phrase "throwing me out" echoed in Samantha's head. That was the phrase Nat had used to describe his separation from Samantha's mom. They had sat down with her and, in an embarrassing re-creation of a paragraph in some child-rearing book about divorce, told her they both loved her and that this separation was between them. That was when her father had said, "Yeah, in other words, your mother is throwing me out."

Samantha knew her father was shy, that he'd be lonely. Tender feelings for him rose up in her. Seeing him in this strange setting made her more sure than ever that he would be miserable, that his heart might break. Her own heart was heavy. She'd just said good-bye to Len.

"How's school going?" asked her father.

"Fine," said Samantha.

They sat in awkward silence, punctuated by an occasional remark, such as, "Do you want to go to lunch?" (Samantha said she had already eaten, though she hadn't) or "What colleges are you looking at?"

Her father showed her around, walking her through the

rooms, explaining things as though conducting a tour for a group of visitors from another planet.

"This is where you'll sleep," he said as he led her into the smaller of the two bedrooms. It was furnished with almond-colored, built-in Formica furniture of the kind used by most large hotel chains. The bedspread and drapes were turquoise and mauve in a splatter pattern, and the carpet was mauve. Opposite the bed, on top of a long, low chest of drawers, was a brand-new TV, complete with a VCR.

Samantha responded in the way she thought her dad expected her to. "Cool, Dad." *This room looks like one at the Hilton,* she thought.

"And this is where you'll take your baths," he said as they walked down a short hallway to the bathroom.

Nat was relieved to be having something to do. He showed her every detail of the building, including the basement, the laundry room and the computerized alarm system. He seemed disappointed when the tour was over and he had shown her the way the vacuum-cleaner hose plugged directly into the wall in each room. That was the last thing on his agenda.

Samantha would, they decided, stay there every Wednesday and Thursday night. She wanted to be in her own house on weekends. She hated the idea of staying with her father. No matter how many of her own things she brought, she knew she wouldn't ever feel at home here. And he was so uneasy around people, even around her, that he made her nervous. She dreaded the whole arrangement, but he looked so miserable already that she didn't want to hurt his feelings. These thoughts occupied her until she came into her own house.

Her mother was still working. She worked until 9:00 on Mondays, and Patty was at a sleepover. Samantha was glad to have the privacy, the silence.

She thought about what she would wear to school the next day. Then she suddenly remembered, with a sharp awareness of anxiety, that Len had left.

She went upstairs to her room. She unfastened her hair from its French braid as she walked into the bathroom to run a bath. Her face in the mirror looked so pale it startled her. She was exhausted and very, very hungry. She sat on the edge of the tub to rest, listening to the water rush into it. After a minute or two, she reached to the ledge for the bottle of bubble bath that Len had given her and poured in a generous amount, filling the small room with the scent of honeysuckle. Then she went to the medicine cabinet, took out her cuticle scissors and looked at them for a long time.

If you suspect that you have a problem, do not wait to get help. The older the habit, the harder it is to shift.

This principle is best expressed by a story. A little girl of four notices that her mother is spending a lot of time in bed. Some days her mother does not even get dressed, but spends the day in her cream-colored robe, the one with the green drawings of Chinese people on bridges all over it. The little girl is scared. The more she sees her mother in that robe in the middle of the day, the more scared she gets.

She asks her granny if there is anything wrong, and her granny tells her that her mother is fine. She asks her father if there is anything wrong with her mother, and he says no. The little girl has no one to talk to about her fears, nowhere to turn.

Her mother has cancer, and no one will tell her.

The little girl eats in secret. She eats amounts of food no one eats in broad daylight. She is chubby at first, but fat at last.

For eight years she keeps asking people if there is anything wrong with her mom, and they keep telling her that there isn't anything wrong, that she should go play. She didn't even know how to play. Or they would say, "Go have something to eat." She knows how to do that.

She eats to calm herself. She eats to soothe her fears. She eats to drown her dread. She eats, also, to please others. She eats to fill the lonely hours.

She can speak of this to no one. Everyone is lying. Cookies are her only friends. She gets fatter and fatter.

This was my story. I was that little girl.

The lesson in this is that you must talk.

Talk to a trusted friend. Talk to a sister or a brother. Talk to a teacher, a guidance counselor, a parent, an e-mail pal. Talk to a journal. Talk to a dog, or to a goldfish. Talk even to yourself.

It took me thirty years to recover from a habit begun in childhood. I don't want that to happen to you.

Talk, and reveal the secrets of your heart, your fears, your sadness and needs.

If you want to talk to a professional listener, good ways to find one are:

1. Ask your guidance counselor to recommend someone.
2. Ask your parent to find a therapist.
3. Ask for a referral from a local mental health clinic.
4. Contact the International Association of Eating Disorder Professionals in Florida at 407-338-6494. They have a directory and can help you find a specialist in your area.

Eve Eliot received both her undergraduate degree in psychology at Queens College and her graduate training in psychology and social work at Queens College, City University of New York; Adelphi and Stonybrook Universities. She worked as a research associate in the department of psychology at the Massachusetts Institute of Technology.

She has certificates of completion in both addiction counseling and eating-disorder counseling programs, and has been trained to use experiential techniques, including psychodrama, to treat trauma survivors. In addition, Eve is the cocreator of

The Eliot-Caplan Method, a new way of treating food addiction, and cofounder of the Menu for Living Weekend Workshops. Please visit her Web site at www.menuforliving.com.

A therapist for the past twelve years, during which time she has treated patients individually and in groups, Eve is also a consultant for The Caron Foundation, where she is a facilitator in their week-long compulsive eating treatment program.

A frequently sought-after expert in the field of food addictions, Eve has appeared on television with Barbara Walters, as well as on radio and local cable shows. She participated in the Choice Opens Our Lives (C.O.O.L.) Project visiting schools to do workshops with students on the topic of eating disorders.

An award-winning advertising copywriter in New York City prior to pursuing her current work in clinical psychology, Eve is the co-author of The Healthy Family Cookbook. She pursued additional training in the field of nutrition, and studied cooking for health at the Kushi Institute in Brookline, Massachusetts.

To reach Eve Eliot, send an e-mail to:

eveliotcounseling@yahoo.com

Our Voices — Our Visions

The stories in the *Teen Ink* Series, written entirely by teens, stick with you—they may leave you in tears, but they will also have you pondering their not-so-obvious conclusions, comparing them to your own life, and remembering times when you felt similar feelings and lived through experiences much like these.

In these books you'll find a forum for your deepest fears, apprehensions, hopes and dreams. Difficulties of life are not only universal, but conquerable, and in a confusing world of seemingly never-ending obstacles, you're never as alone as you may think.

Teen Ink
Our Voices, Our Visions
Code #8164 • Quality Paperback • $12.95

Teen Ink 2
More Voices, More Visions
Code #9136 • Quality Paperback • $12.95

...Relationships...
...Friendships...
Read about them...

Bestselling author Kim Kirberger combines her heartfelt advice with stories and letters from teens to bring you this great series. Love, crushes, breakups; best friends, cliques, growing and learning . . . it's all here!

Teen Love: On Relationships
Code #7346 • Quality Paperback • $12.95

Teen Love: On Friendship
Code #8156 • Quality Paperback • $12.95

...Write about them!

Bound to become invaluable keepsakes! Filled with quizzes, exercises and other teens' experiences, these journals give you the space to record your thoughts, feelings, and fears.

A Journal on Relationships
Code #7664 • Quality Paperback • $12.95

A Journal on Friendship
Code #9128 • Quality Paperback • $12.95